New-Fashioned Grand-Parenting

Changing America One Grandchild at a Time

Julie Nelson

New-Fashioned Grand-Parenting

Changing America One Grandchild at a Time

Julia Nelson

Foreword by Dr. Arthur Kornhaber, M.D.

Allyn Group Publications
Delaware, OH

Copyright © 1999 Julia Nelson
Printed and bound in the United States of America. All rights reserved.

No part of this book may be reproduced or transmitted in any form or by any means, electronic or mechanical, including photocopying, recording, or by an information storage and retrieval system—except by a reviewer who may quote brief passages in a review to be printed in a magazine or newspaper—without permission in writing from the publisher. For information, contact: Allyn Group Publications, P. O. Box 1116, Delaware, OH 43015–8116.

This book contains information gathered from many sources which is intended for general reference. It is sold with the understanding that neither the author or publisher is engaged in rendering any legal, psychological or other professional advice. The publisher and author disclaim any personal liability for advice or information presented within. We assume no responsibility for errors, inaccuracies, omissions, or any inconsistency herein. Any slights of people, places, or organizations are unintentional.

First printing 1999.
Edited by Pamela Allen-Goad

Publisher's Cataloging-in-Publication
(Provided by Quality Books, Inc.)

Nelson, Julia.
  New-fashioned grandparenting : changing America one grandchild at a time / Julia Nelson ; foreword by Arthur Kornhaber. -- 1st ed.
   p. cm.
  Includes bibliographical references and index
  LCCN: 99-64476
  ISBN: 0-9673230-0-2

  1. Grandparenting. 2. Moral education.
  I. Title

HQ759.9.N45 1999   306.874'5
                           QBI99-974

ACKNOWLEDGMENTS

Many thanks to family, friends and neighbors who helped along the way. Nancy Woodall and Anne Ritter tackled the first version and provided lots of productive suggestions. JoAnn Crombie served me a great cup of coffee at my favorite bookstore and suggested the name of a local editor. Pamela Allen-Goad put up with a first-time author and completed the editing chores just before giving birth to her first baby, a lovely girl. My layout specialist, Sharon Landers, was discovered with the help of David Fleming.

I am grateful for the enthusiastic support of friends in Argentina where much of the writing took place.

From the beginning, my husband provided every kind of help and support. He listened carefully to my ideas and shared his own. He helped me wrestle the computer into submission every now and then and took over many times when I could not prevail. I gained from his professional expertise and utilized books from his collection. He endured my frustrations and shared my excitement as the material came together.

And most of all, my love and thanks to the grandchildren who brought all of this about.

AUTHOR'S INVITATION

Please share your comments, ideas, experiences, suggestions and questions. I would love to hear from you.

Write to the author, Julia Nelson, in care of the publisher:

Allyn Group Publications
P.O. Box 1116
Deleware, OH 43015-8116
or
E-mail: allyngrouppub@midohio.net

TABLE OF CONTENTS

Foreword viii
Preface ix
Introduction xi

PART ONE: GRANDPARENTS AS ENTREPRENEURS 1
   CHAPTER 1. Modern Realities 9
   CHAPTER 2. Finding Common Ground 19
   CHAPTER 3. The Challenge 25

PART TWO: A NEW JOB DESCRIPTION 33
   CHAPTER 4. The Business Analogy 35
   CHAPTER 5. The Franchise Alternative 40

PART THREE: MARKET RESEARCH 45
   CHAPTER 6. Macroanalysis—the Big Picture 47
   CHAPTER 7. Microanalysis—the Local Snapshot 57

PART FOUR: VALUES AND BEHAVIORS 65
   CHAPTER 8. Values Orientation 66
   CHAPTER 9. *The Three C's* 71
   CHAPTER 10. Self-Control 84
   CHAPTER 11. Freedom and Responsibility 91

PART FIVE: BUSINESS PLANNING 99
   CHAPTER 12. The Mission Statement 100
   CHAPTER 13. Consulting and Leadership 102
   CHAPTER 14. Management Skills 113
   CHAPTER 15. Business Philosophy 121

PART SIX: CLIENT EVALUATION 127
   CHAPTER 16. Human Development 128
   CHAPTER 17. Development in Childhood 135
   CHAPTER 18. Development in Youth 139
   CHAPTER 19. Development in Early Adolescence ... 143
   CHAPTER 20. Development in Late Adolescence 146
   CHAPTER 21. Research and Record Keeping 150

PART SEVEN: CUSTOMER SERVICE 155
    CHAPTER 22. Customer Relations 156
    CHAPTER 23. Praise and Criticism 172

PART EIGHT: *THE BIRTHDAY PROGRAM* 187
    CHAPTER 24. Rituals 188
    CHAPTER 25. Origins of *The Birthday Program* ... 192
    CHAPTER 26. Getting Started 196
    CHAPTER 27. On-the-Job Training 200
    CHAPTER 28. *My Book of Birthdays* 216

PART NINE: *THE BUSINESS OF LIFE* 221
    CHAPTER 29. Working in the Real World 222
    CHAPTER 30. Grandparents at Work 226

A Complete Job Description for *The Business of Life* 229

References 231

Index 240

Order Form 242

IMAGINE EXERCISES

Exercise 1. **The Entrepreneur** 28
Exercise 2. **The Slingshot** 59
Exercise 3. **Leadership** 106
Exercise 4. **Interviewing** 119
Exercise 5. **Respect** 159
Exercise 6. **The Actor** 209

FOREWORD

In *New-Fashioned Grandparenting* author Julia Nelson shows us an innovative and creative way to be better grandparents. [She] uses an entrepreneurial model *(The Business of Life)* and applies it to a practical "delivery" system for transferring one's wisdom and experience to grandchildren. The transfer takes place through a consistent, reliable and predictable methodology called *The Birthday Program.*

This book will be very helpful, practical, and informative for all grandparents. And especially those who have been caught off balance by the maelstrom of personal, familial and social changes they have experienced throughout their lives; forces that can hinder effective grandparenting.

> Dr. Arthur Kornhaber, M.D., is a child psychiatrist, researcher, author of several books on grandparenting, and the President/Founder of the Foundation for Grandparenting based in Ojai, CA.

PREFACE

This book, *New-Fashioned Grandparenting,* is a how-to book that was prompted neither by academic requirements nor by scholarly research but by personal distress. I wrestled with questions that may be familiar to you. How in the world does grandparenting work in this society? How do we deal with the geographic distances between family members or the emotional distances caused by divorce? How much time do you have to devote to grandparenting? What does the role mean in this day and age?

My expectations about grandparenting were initially very modest, but I really did some serious thinking when the new generation in my family reached toddler stage and they began to be especially interesting to me as individuals. At that point, I realized that my knowledge of them would come in the form of long-distance reports from their parents. The same parents who were much too busy to keep me up to date. Then it dawned on me that they were not going to know who I was either. I felt utterly cheated.

I couldn't and didn't want to retract the mutual decision that took my husband and I first to another state and then gave us the chance to live and work in Argentina. These moves brought both of us wonderful new opportunities and new experiences. But none of them had anything to do with grandparenting. I admit that I was stuck for a while in simple self-pity. Then, I began to read and to think. I have had a lifelong habit of refusal to accept lemons when I could just as well make lemonade or lemon meringue pie, for that matter. Before long that will reasserted itself and I began to contemplate possibilities.

This book came from the substance of my life, from my inclination to analyze systems or situations, and to design plans in response. It came from my experience as a small business owner and the discovery that I enjoy selling something I understand and believe in. My long interest in the intricacies of successful human communication played a part, as did my perpetual curiosity about the changes in America's social structures over time, and about our efforts to understand the human mind and our own behavior. Even my delight in learning about ancient peoples of the earth and the rituals and ceremonies of those cultures found a place in my thinking.

I would describe my self as an ordinary, reasonably well-educated American and, darn it, I needed to solve this grandparenting dilemma so I could feel good again and look forward to ... well, something that I hadn't yet defined.

Now, it is certainly possible to find books on the subject of grandparenting and there is good advice available. The difficulty comes in trying to put the advice into practice. It tends to be a hit-or-miss proposition. There are bits and pieces of information that never congeal into something that gives me the certainty of, "Ah, yes. Now, that's really grandparenting and I can do it!"

I concluded that it was time to shake things up just a bit.

And that is how I became determined to create a solution that would work for me. I knew that I needed to make grandparenting a meaningful part of real life so that I would know my grandchildren and they would know me. Once I had designed the format, it dawned on me that it could just as well work for others. My solution, *The Birthday Program,* is something that I now believe will bring hope and excitement to grandparents everywhere.

It's simple, it's easy, and you can do it just as well as I can. Why am I so confident? Because we mature adults, as unique and individual as we are, have become specialists in the subject of life. We have the wisdom, the experience, and the skills needed to talk about what really matters.

When millions of us grandparents, all across this country, are going about the business of being new-fashioned, the importance of our role in this society will become abundantly apparent.

Julia Nelson, 1999

INTRODUCTION

Who will be interested in this book?

Many grandparents report enjoying their grandchildren thoroughly on a regular basis. Some grandparents get involved intermittently on special occasions. Some are retired and others are busy working. There are those who are skateboarding with grandchildren and those who aren't about to try. Many of us simply live too far apart for regular interaction. More and more of us are filling that gap by using e-mail. This book is for every one of you wherever you live and whatever your particular circumstances.

The bottom line here is that most grandparents want to help their grandchildren become good people. There is an impulse to use what we have learned about life for the benefit of the next generation. This book speaks to that impulse.

It's time we put grandparenting on the cutting edge. Society needs our wisdom, our judgement and our values. If that sounds like a very old-fashioned idea to you, you're right. It is. The new focus, presented in this book, is in the method—not the message.

I suggest that we tap into the modern outlook of entrepreneurs, make use of a set of contemporary skills used by consultants, give ourselves a specific job title and get down to business.

This business has nothing whatsoever to do with money. It's all about creating a demand for your skills and experience. We live at a time when marketing is king. We can brush up our image by adopting a new style. Let's show how authentic grandparenting, with traditional content, can be a new-fashioned activity. This book will show you how to participate—how to help your grandchildren become good people—in a way that's fun as well as serious. Let's go for it!

PART ONE

GRANDPARENTS AS ENTREPRENEURS

What is the world's oldest unpaid profession? Throughout human history younger generations have turned to their elders for information, advice, encouragement, and support. Many grandparents look at their adult children when they become new parents and recall that old saying, "If only I had known then what I know now." They realize that as new parents they were once untested and unprepared for the full realities of raising children. It took long years and lots of learning to develop those parenting skills and gain confidence in child rearing. Now, as grandparents, they recognize that if first-time parents came equipped with this knowledge, then the raising of children would be done by people of experience and expertise, that is, by professionals.

I wonder how you are making use of your skills and talents, your wisdom and experience, to enrich the lives of your grandchildren. Do you live a charmed life? Is it possible that no one in your family network has divorced? Do you see your grandchildren regularly and fully participate in their lives? Do you search for any evidence of a generation gap as you interact with their parents? Are you confident that your grandchildren live in a safe, secure world? What a dream this would be! If it were real, I would find it easy to imagine that you were fulfilling your ideal role as a

GRANDPARENTS AS ENTREPRENEURS

professional expert in the art of living and that your grandchildren were thriving under your guidance. You would be a well-respected elder, and you would be busy contributing to the development of a new generation of fine Americans. But I doubt very much that you are living such a life.

You and I have been cast in a rigid mold and shelved. We're dust catchers unless we care to baby-sit or produce presents or finance college funds. Oh sure, we do those things and more and do them willingly, but none of them come close to recognizing or tapping into the wealth of expertise that we possess. We go along with things the way they are even though we are cut off from a full role in society. We are left feeling generally ignored and useless.

Take a stand with me and just say, "No, my life is worth more than this."

In the third stage of life we become invisible because we are not expected to be productive. That conclusion is superficial, based on a thoughtless assumption that there is no longer anything of importance that we can do. I contend that we have a major job assignment that calls for our own particular brand of expertise.

While I have no intention of becoming a completely somber and serious grandparent, I do want to spend some time in a meaningful and vital activity. I want to make a difference in this world, in a small way, beginning with my own grandchildren. This is a dream that you and I can share, and it is a dream that we can make come true.

For many reasons, the traditional pattern of transferring skills and wisdom from one generation to the next no longer applies to modern living. At the close of the Victorian era when the nineteenth century became the new twentieth century, the patriarchal family structure ensured that standards and skills were passed down to new family members from the oldest people in the extended family. This pattern was supported by the proximity of family members who often shared the typical agrarian lifestyle of that period. Most families lived on farms or in small communities where they interacted daily with cousins, aunts and uncles, and grandparents, as well as with siblings and parents. Values and behavior standards were generally shared and endorsed by everyone within the

Introduction

family as well as the other residents of the community. There were few connections to and few intrusions from the outside world. At that time, there existed a shared and familiar assumption of the function of grandparenting. There was no need to question or examine the role because grandparenting was an ordinary, natural part of everyday life. The knowledge and skills of the elders were very much in demand. That was the nature of old-fashioned grandparenting.

How do we define or describe a contemporary grandparent? Today, there is no standard model for grandparenting. The family structure is now characterized by variety. Generations are often separated by time and space; individuals are influenced by an enormous range of media sources, and communities are rarely cohesive. How, then, can we define the most suitable role for grandparents as we approach another century?

We already know that in the twenty-first century there will be a multitude of individuals who technically qualify for the title of grandparent. Not only will there be many new grandparents, but also numerous great-grandparents, many great-great grandparents, and a contingent of step-grandparents. Together, these people are the elders of our society. Can this group of elders, despite its diversity, be defined by a common function? Can our society directly benefit from their expertise? In order to answer these questions, we must discover more about who the members of this group are and the professional credentials they will have to offer.

Most of these people, based on their experiences while growing up, would be able to describe what a grandparent is and what one does. Personal points of view are to be expected. Yet within these generations there exists quite a range of opinions on the preferred style and substance of grandparenting. Surprisingly, there is no shared, fundamental consensus on a definition.

By questioning many individuals, we would collect a list of attributes and a variety of particulars that would more or less cover the range of things that grandparents do and that might indicate those ways in which grandparents are thought to be important. If we were to categorize these grandparenting functions and to arrange a priority ranking, would the most crucial factor appear at the top of the list? Of all the things that

GRANDPARENTS AS ENTREPRENEURS

grandparents do and like and want to do, I prefer to concentrate on the one element that distinguishes this role from others in the family structure.

The fundamental business of life for all species is to replicate themselves in order to guarantee their survival. The ultimate challenge for us humans is to replicate our humanity, and that is the essence of grandparenting. What do we forfeit, as a society, if we lose the most crucial knowledge that our elders possess?

It has been suggested that grandparents are a cultural bridge that links the older generation to the newest by transmitting our important cultural principles. In this sense, grandparenting is not unlike the teaching of cultural literacy. I believe it would be even more precise to describe grandparents as the keepers of our cultural conscience.

We, the elders of society, are the guides who have the template. All together, we possess vast resources of knowledge, skills, and wisdom which must no longer be ignored or wasted. It is even more important now to recognize that we are the people who exemplify primary American values that are in danger of being lost or corrupted.

Do you remember hearing the slogan, "This is not your father's Oldsmobile," from a television ad campaign of a few years ago? The ad emphasized a sleek, modern, youthful automobile clearly aimed to attract new, young buyers. It was still the same brand, but it was a bit different. In the same way, this guidebook will look at grandparenting and bring its heart and soul into focus. That focus will be transformed into a simple activity that any grandparent can perform. This activity will call upon the wisdom and skills that adults have acquired and treat them as professional credentials. Then these skills will be put to good use for the benefit of our grandchildren's generation. Just like that slogan, grandparenting will be the same, but a little bit different. You won't be driving your father's Oldsmobile or your grandfather's Model T; you will be a new-fashioned grandparent!

American society, by virtue of its rapidly changing family structure and social culture, has created a job opportunity that calls for a response from the ranks of those who grew up with commonly shared values. Although there is a clear need for grandparents to become involved in their grandchildren's lives, no formalized system for doing so has yet been proposed or developed. It is time to recognize the need, to accept the challenge, and to get down to the true business of grandparenting in a thoroughly practical way. We must update the historical responsibility of transmitting basic cultural values, our collective conscience, and our humanity to the next generation.

Consider the Dagara of West Africa. In that culture, ". . . old age and childhood are held to be the important times of life, the times when one does great work. Children and the elders, being chronologically closer to the spirit world, hang out together and discuss the meaning of life. The others are seen as more or less taking up space as they provide the manual labor that sustains the village."[1] This picturesque image is from a series of articles on retirement found in a popular American investment magazine. The author speculates that the coming together of the very old and the very young is one of the lifestyle changes that may occur as the proportion of mature adults increases dramatically in our own population. Will we, in our own variation of Dagaran society, find it more and more natural for the elders and the young to coalesce for caretaking, nurturing, and sharing?

What Can Grandparents Do?

Most of us have heard an adult acknowledge a special childhood experience. The memory involves a time when a trusted, older person spoke a few simple words of wisdom. The speaker might have been a family member, a teacher, or even a famous person making a public speech. The adult remembers a simple, yet inspirational, lesson that the older person provided. This lesson was so direct and profound that it remained influential throughout the life of the recipient. Such people often express gratitude years later for the positive changes that that bit of wisdom made in their lives.

People who have such memories always claim that those words have been a constant guide. We can tell by listening to them that they are revealing a significant event that had a lasting impact on their thinking from that time on. The circumstances may have been humble, but the words actually affected their entire lives.

Let's listen in on a conversation that is taking place in Happy Valley, USA, right now.

A CONSULTATION WITH DYLAN

Setting: a quiet bedroom in his parents' home. It is early spring.

Participants: Dylan, age eight, Grandmother, ageless, and Grandfather, who is running interference so that the conversation will not be interrupted.

The occasion: A long-distance trip made by the grandparents to visit family. This visit takes place almost two months following Dylan's birthday.

The fact that this consultation takes place close to his birthday is an important point because Grandmother is practicing The Birthday Program.

Action: As Dylan bounces into the room and flops onto one of the twin beds, Grandma arranges herself Indian-style on the opposite bed.

Grandmother: "Dylan, I'm so glad to see you! At last we can have our special talk! Do you remember when I called you on the phone on your eighth birthday?" Dylan nods. "And I sang 'Happy birthday to you, happy birthday to you' (Grandmother sings the song through), and you giggled?" Dylan grins and giggles again.

Grandmother: "I wish I could have been right here with you then. But I'm here now and I want to know about all the things you discovered last year. Tell me about the citizenship award that you received at school. What does it mean?"

Dylan (frowning): "Um, I forgot."

Grandmother: "Well, citizenship is a pretty big word that grownups use. I think this award must mean that you did something right and that you set a good example at school. Did the principal talk about the way you act when you're there?"

Dylan (looking bright and lively): "Oh, now I remember! She said that I act nice to people and, uh … I take care of things."

Grandmother (nodding): "I see. Those things are very good, and I'm happy to hear that you behave that way. You treat teachers and other kids with respect, and you treat school property with care. Is that a good description?"

Dylan (nodding): "Yup."

Grandmother: "Those are examples of good citizenship. Now, let me ask you another question about this: What's a litter bug?"

Introduction

Dylan (grinning again): "A person who throws junk 'n' stuff out the window."

Grandmother: "You mean like tossing hamburger wrappers and paper cups out of the car window?" (Dylan nods.) "Is that a good way to act? Would that be an example of good or poor citizenship?"

Dylan: "It's bad, Gramma. You shouldn't do it!"

Grandmother: "You're right. And that's what I call poor citizenship. People in our family are NOT litter bugs. We believe that each person should put waste paper in the proper place and help keep the streets and sidewalks and grass clean. That's part of good citizenship, just like taking care of the things you use at school. Now you have two examples of citizenship to think about."

Grandmother takes out a spiral notebook and a pen and makes some notes.

At the top of the page, there is a list of topics and issues that she wants to work into the discussion. These topics are based on Dylan's experiences of the past year. Grandmother is both listening for and introducing examples of "The Three 'C's" which represent Character, Civility, and Citizenship.

Dylan: "Hey, what're you doing?"

Grandmother: "I'm making a record of the things we're talking about. Later I'll put them in an album and keep them. Now, there's something I'd like to know. What . . . ?

Dylan (interrupting): "Okay, Grandma, now write this down." (Grandmother grins this time and the conversation continues).

The album that is referred to here is called My Book of Birthdays *which was developed specifically for use with* The Birthday Program.

We will listen in on more of these consultations as Grandmother practices using *The Birthday Program*. This interactive program was designed so that each of us can create and manage a predictable pattern of opportunities for finding evidence of important life skills, appropriate behaviors, and good values in the lives of our own grandchildren.

Why leave this vitally important act of sharing to chance? If a few well-chosen words, shared on a single occasion, can have a meaningful impact on someone's life, then it must be wise to intentionally create an opportunity to say them. This bit of inspiration became the foundation for everything you will find in this book.

If you are a modern grandparent, you may be thinking that you live too far away from your grandchildren or that you are too busy working and too tired to think about something new. These things are true for many of us. Therefore, any system that we might organize for purposeful grandparent/grandchild conversations must be practical and manageable for everyone.

Conversely, you may live very close to your grandchildren so that you see and enjoy them regularly. Why should you consider doing things any differently? The answer is this: because with frequent contact, we often fail to notice the small things that really count. We miss opportunities just because we are so busy that we aren't focused on looking for them.

What if we all were to work together to mold something new from a role that is now old-fashioned? We all have a title, grandparent. If this is a professional position, why don't we have a clear job description? Where is our training manual?

What Is the Scope of This Book?

In this book, you will find the answers to your questions about why and how, and we will even discuss where and when. You will not be expected to give up or change any part of grandparenting that you currently enjoy. You will be invited to think like an entrepreneur in order to bring modern concepts to our grandparenting role and to address the needs of modern children. The goal is to share our wisdom, knowledge, and values through crafted conversations, one-on-one, with our own grandchildren.

I will propose a method that will allow us to work together independently and a *Mission Statement* that will focus and define our new strategy. A symbolic business plan will be outlined giving grandparents the role of consultants. Because our "clients" are growing children, we will review our knowledge of child development. As professionals, we must possess a skill base in order to perform effectively.

Once we are informed and prepared, we will explore in greater depth this unique consulting initiative called *The Birthday Program,* and prepare for typical, real-life problems and difficulties. Finally, we will anticipate some of the benefits of the process for your grandchildren and for you.

When we put this activity into practice, grandparenting will become synonymous with the basic business of life. Thereafter, as grandparents, you and I can expect to be viewed as skilled professionals and as valuable partners who have a clear role within the modern family.

CHAPTER 1. Modern Realities

The title *grandparent* is one that we use to identify the older members of the family, but for most of our history these folks weren't actually alive for very long. An American child born in 1776, for example, would not expect to live much beyond the age of 35. People in the mid-eighteenth century were actually near the end of their lives at the stage when many couples are now starting their families. Of course, there were exceptions, but there was not really much incentive to make elaborate plans for one's declining years.[1]

Even at the beginning of the twentieth century, the stage of life that we now casually consider to be middle age was actually old age. Indeed, life expectancy was only 50 years at that time. Some experts predict that by about 2040, the life span will be 75 years for men and 83 for women. Other analysts project even higher numbers.[2]

Around the world, people are rapidly developing an entirely different view of grandparenting and old age.

How Have our Lifestyles Changed?

We will remember the twentieth century as a time of breathtaking advances in nutrition, health care, medicine, and medical technology, all of which contributed to the continuing evolution and changing definition of old age. We have acclimated so rapidly to these marvels that our society generally dismisses the whole issue of grandparenting right along with the very notion of getting old. We persist in refusing to acknowledge such an outcome for youth and vigor. Not only our health and beauty industries, but our genetic research companies as well, devote extensive time and money to the goal of pushing youth and middle age as far into the future as humanly and scientifically possible. Already we have learned to expect repair or replacement of faulty body parts as we strive to retain our youthful physical capacities. This devotion to health and youthfulness can be an asset for active grandparents who project a new image of silver-haired vitality. However, because this image does not coincide with previous expectations about what grandparents are like and what they do, there is some confusion regarding the definition of the grandparenting role. People no longer look or act like grandparents when we think that they should.

In many cultures around the world, the elders are still revered and honored. This attitude represents a traditional way of thinking about the status of their older members. In contrast, our own culture, which once shared that tradition, now celebrates youth and achievement as the high points of merit and respect.

This youthful focus yields a certain amount of confusion for modern adults. In many ways, the image that we have of grandparents and our expectations about grandparenting are still lodged in tradition, and therefore, our assumptions are based on what old people once did at the end of their lives. However, that picture has been so blurred that it is no longer accurate. Many of these same people, who not long ago would have been considered old, now have typical adult expectations for themselves that coincide with the prime of adulthood, such as productivity, creativity, adventure, challenge, and opportunity. These expectations are not compatible with rocking chairs. The traditional concept of grandparenting no longer feels like a natural or comfortable fit.

In many ways, we are functionally dissociated from the former role expectations yet we still acquire the title and status of grandparents. As a result, we wonder how we are supposed to act. Just what are we supposed to do and what can be expected of us when we are busy working and living a full adult life? Many of us have several roles and separate identities that coexist, making it difficult to distinguish grandparenting as a separate and unique activity. We find ourselves making adjustments in order to accommodate conflicting demands on our time and, as a result, grandparenting has become just one of the numerous options in our busy lives. That makes the role sound trivial; unfortunately, for many adults it is all too true. Grandparenting is just one of many choices.

It is apparent to me that modern grandparenting, in order to survive as a distinct function, must more clearly suit the self-image, the mental outlook, and the lifestyles of young middle-aged adults. And yet, having stated this, a great deal of complexity remains.

For example, what is the definition of middle age? Various proposals have been suggested that carve new age segments out of the life span, yet there are variations among the analysts with no consensus in sight. You might agree that middle age, or middle adulthood, now extends from about 50 years to perhaps 64, and that late adulthood begins at 65 and lasts until age 79 or so. Old age would begin at 80 years.[3] On the other hand, there are those who believe that middle age is a state of mind and, therefore, entirely an individual and subjective definition. As the boundaries of truly old age are extended, some suggest that 70 years of age now marks the conclusion of the middle period. Precision on this matter can be left to statisticians and others who analyze populations or to those who develop programs and policies that will affect this growing segment of society. Of more importance here is the way in which we define and categorize ourselves and the realities behind the decisions that we make about our own lives.

How Has Grandparenting Evolved?

Do you realize that there are many different points of view among older Americans concerning just what the role of a grandparent is all about? Debate and disagreement over its meaning isn't new. Grandparenting has been analyzed and evaluated for several decades as our family structure has changed.

Dr. Arthur Kornhaber, for example, is known for his firm and vocal stance in favor of fully involved grandparenting. His recommendations are supported by original research undertaken with colleagues and published in the early 1980s. The research subjects were children from diverse ethnic and socioeconomic backgrounds. These youngsters demonstrated in words and pictures that they knew what grandparents should be and what they should do. Many of the children described an ideal; others described real people. You and I would recognize all of the routine, daily activities as well as those special times with grandchildren that would represent the ideal image of grandparenting within family life at mid-century.[4]

What could be more fundamental and convincing than a direct report from the recipients of grandparenting? Even children who did not have grandparents knew what they were missing.

Another specialist, Dr. Fitzhugh Dodson, who published his views on the circumstances that began to affect grandparenting in the second half of this century, suggested that most grandparents, even those having a wonderful time in the role, could improve if they learned more about the skills needed to be effective. Grandparents were advised to make use of child psychology and modern teaching methods to improve on the tendency to simply do what came naturally.[5]

Our knowledge and understanding about child development has grown along with the changes that have occurred in the American family structure. Since the 1950s we have experienced a rapid shift from a rural to an urban society, increasing numbers of women in the work force, a growing rate of divorce, and a much greater mobility of families. By the mid-eighties, the generation gap that seemed to have widened between parents and children was making it increasingly difficult to reach a common consensus on how the next generation should be raised. The gap between grandchildren and grandparents also grew. Grandparents, being thoroughly old-fashioned, were generally viewed as even more irrelevant and dull than parents. Grandparents themselves weren't in agreement about the meaning of their role in family life.

Why Don't All Grandparents Share a Common Point of View?

People in every age group, or generation, exhibit a splendid variety of skills and talents, of formal and informal training and expertise, of education and knowledge. Our individuality is expressed in many ways. At the same time, there are broad generalizations that seem to define generations. The incredible events and changes of twentieth-century living have helped to create pronounced clusters of events and experiences that serve to identify and distinguish the generations. We have a penchant for labeling and categorizing each of them, and we tend to think that they are distinct and discrete.

Each of us finds a comfortable sense of place among those who shared our own youthful experiences. Each group has shared reference points in time. From music, clothing, and automobile styles to attitudes and expectations, we identify with our peers, and apparently this perspective is retained even as we grow older. These memories and preferences help to define a part of who we are and give us a sense of belonging. Sociologists and population analysts call these groupings *age cohorts*. Many readers have become familiar with this concept through the popular writing of Gail Sheehy in her books on life's passages. Her first effort on this topic, *Passages: Mapping Your Life Across Time*, was widely read and set the stage for succeeding volumes on growth stages in adult development.

Various names have been used by researchers and authors to identify the cohort segments. As you read through the following descriptions, remember that the information that I have included was purposely selected in order to focus on attitudes about maturity and retirement. You should recognize the attributes of your generation. It is true that these groupings are generalities and that there is much blending during the transition from one generation to another because the cohort demarcations are arbitrary. And yet, for a broad view of predominant tendencies, these cohorts reveal some distinct and interesting patterns according to the authors of *Lifetrends,* whose work (subtitled, *The Future of Baby Boomers and Other Aging Americans*[6]) is referenced in the following cohort descriptions.

The group of elders born early in this century, now great-grandparents, suffered through the Great Depression and have been quiet and cautious in their old age. They have a particular distinction because some of them became the first residents of the early planned retirement communities. These were the grandparents who took a definite step away from easy, regular involvement with other family members and grandchildren. By physically and permanently moving to a new location which did not allow children, they chose to break with tradition. These people clearly put a barrier—physical distance—between themselves and their progeny.

A new level of affluence and education marks the next cohort, many of whom fought in World War II. They are also more assertive. This generation has made the American Association of Retired Persons a lobbying powerhouse. They are often characterized as having made so many sacrifices for their children that they have tended to take advantage of opportunities to enjoy life once they retired. Many have taken to the road in their recreational vehicles, some with bumper stickers announcing that they are spending their children's inheritance. Their attitude is one of non-interference with the raising of their grandchildren. This group put a new barrier—emotional distance—between themselves and their families and limitations on the kind of involvement that could occur.

The group that came of age in the 1950s is often referred to as the silent generation. This is the source of the robot-like man in the gray flannel suit, that dutiful fellow who followed the rules and blended into the woodwork. Growing up during a time of relative political and social calm when everyone settled into the suburbs, this generation began to enjoy the affluence that followed World War II. This period marks the time when the suburbs and isolated nuclear families began to multiply rapidly. It became ever more likely that the family took an automobile ride to visit grandparents who lived alone and lived longer than in previous generations.

Overall, as teenagers, this cohort conformed to adult expectations. Although several individuals from this generation, like Elvis, Abbie Hoffman, and Gloria Steinem, helped set the stage for social change, this generation isn't expected to impact the grandparenting role in any major way, according to the *Lifetrend* authors. In dramatic contrast, the Baby Boomers are expected to change just about everything as they age.

Americans' attention turned to the Baby Boomers' needs due to the enormous number of children who were born between 1946 and 1964. This population segment totals some 78 million individuals, and we are all well aware that the Boomers created a distinct youth culture and a disdain for anyone older than 30. Grandparenting got a bad rap.

Because there were so many youngsters being educated in unusually large class sizes, the authors surmised that they tended to look to their peers for guidance and direction rather than to their elders. This pattern of group consensus accounts for some of the predictions made about the kinds of change they may initiate during their tenure as senior citizens. In contrast to great-grandparents, who more often sacrificed for their children, the Boomer parents tended to give their dual careers first priority. Mothers in this cohort are almost assumed to be employees and many are now opting for business ownership. In fact, due to advances in birth control methods, the Boomers were able to delay childbearing while they acquired extra education, careers, and the consumer goods that make life comfortable. One eventual outcome of this trend is that they will find themselves grandparenting at an older stage of their lives. It also appears likely that they will find themselves faced with the simultaneous need to care for their own elderly parents.

Predictions from *Lifetrends* for retirement lifestyles and attitudes based on the experiences and expectations of the Boomer cohort include: a possible return to communal living in later years characterized by housing shared among several generations of women, an end to early retirement, elder care for the Boomers' parents, continued consumer influence, more emphasis on preventive medicine, and some interesting possibilities for the future of grandparenting. The authors hypothesize that the Boomers may come to regret how little time they spent with their own children and become enthusiastic grandparents.

These cohort definitions provide us with a general framework for considering the variety of views on and expectations of the grandparenting role today and some sense of their origins.

What Else Has Affected the Grandparenting Role?

Many of the books that I have found about grandparenting, written by my elders, have recommended a supportive, gentle style of participation. In this view, grandparents should stay in the background of family life. They should respond when called upon by their children, but are cautioned against initiating any intrusion. These publications endorse a clear preference for a hands-off policy which leaves raising children up to the parents. I have found only a few experts who advocate a more "traditional" approach which encourages a full range of involvement. This approach is the one which provides us with the folks who are most easily recognized as grandparents and who are often viewed with a sense of nostalgia.

Based on the books available that address grandparenting, it is clear to me that the attitudes and recommendations of the authors have been influenced by the prevailing social attitudes of their day.

GRANDPARENTS AS ENTREPRENEURS

Of course, as individuals, each of us is influenced not only by our own generation-based circumstances but also by other lifestyle changes that occur as we mature and raise our own families. The rate of divorce in the second half of this century has created fractured families and reconstituted families at a stunning rate. The resulting convoluted relationships all too frequently leave grandparents on the outside of the new family structure, longing to be participants. In extreme cases, the court system now deals with issues revolving around the legal visitation rights of grandparents.

Many adults find themselves living a significant distance from their own offspring. Frequently it is the children who have moved on in order to pursue better employment opportunities, but it is now almost as likely that the grandparents themselves have done the moving. Divorce often plays a role in the scattering of family members, as well. These dual forces, divorce and distance, create enormous challenges for the very concept of grandparenting. Some of us find it realistic to let go and others struggle to remain connected. Some are relieved to be unburdened, while others suffer a deep loss.

Grandparenting today can be described as a matter of individual personality, age cohort, distance from family members, family divisions resulting from divorce, plus the type and quality of grandparenting which each of us experienced as a youngster. Other influences might have included ethnic or cultural heritage and religious training. This mixture produced in each of us either a primarily positive, negative, or indifferent attitude toward the role. Some of us have beloved role models to live up to while others will need to be creative.

Right now, every individual grandparent's role is altogether a matter of personal definition having been influenced by all or many of these factors. This murky picture illustrates the nebulous condition of American grandparenting. It is terribly unclear and is lacking any coherent consensus. If nothing else, its current variability does confirm our fundamental belief in individuality.

What About You?

How would you describe yourself as a grandparent or as someone who expects to be a grandparent? If you were challenged to be the best grandparent that you could be, how would you describe yourself? Who would be your role model? Did you learn significant lessons about life from one or more of your own grandparents? Perhaps there were things that you now realize were learned indirectly by virtue of their everyday presence in your life. Maybe you remember specific things that they shared with you. On the other hand, there may be things that you feel you missed out on and you may remember envying other youngsters. What does grandparenting mean to you now and how will you fill the role?

There are lively and charming books available that review activities and opportunities for the companionship that grandparenting can provide just as there are references to the reduction of distances through conversing with one's grandchildren via E-mail. These things are not insignificant; they are part of the mixture of techniques and preferences that individuals bring to the role. However, there are more fundamental questions to be addressed if we intend to join forces and make a meaningful impact on many, many young lives.

How Do You View Your Life Now?

It is not unusual for people who find themselves in their early to mid-fifties to discover and welcome a sense of contentment and satisfaction with their lives. Many enjoy a surge of self-confidence in their ability to deal with things and, therefore, to feel more at ease with life. There is less need to prove yourself capable because much has already been accomplished. Those things which truly matter have been identified and the rest is more likely to be ignored. Experience has revealed that setbacks can be overcome and that multiple options are frequently available. These factors converge in a sense of having achieved maturity and a kind of rest period follows. This oasis has been called the *Age of Mastery* by author Sheehy, who believes that it falls roughly between the ages of 45 and 65. It can be a wonderful time of life, she wrote in *New Passages,* for "at last we humans have the chance to show what feats of mind and spirit our species might be capable of once freed from the humdrum activities of survival, reproduction, family care, and perhaps even full-time jobs."[7]

The period of mental relaxation and self-assurance sometimes gives way to a somewhat surprising impulse to reconsider philosophical issues that may not have been prominent since teen years. Perhaps there is simply more time to contemplate fundamental questions from the new perspective of middle age. In certain quiet moments we may feel the need to consider our place in the flow of time. We may wonder anew why we are here, what can and should be accomplished in our remaining life span, and whether or not we have fulfilled our purpose. Fame and fortune may seem a little less important and are often replaced by an unwillingness to arrive at old age filled with regrets.

In the midst of this period, and especially with the arrival of grandchildren, there is frequently a change of focus. With our wants and needs substantially fulfilled, time gives us the opportunity to look to the needs of others. There is often an impulse to want to be remembered, to leave something of ourselves behind, and to feel that we have made a difference in ways that satisfy the soul.

These impulses can lead to a life stage described by psychologist Erik Erikson as one of *generativity*. Generativity defines people who have found a basic sense of satisfaction with their past achievements and who begin looking for ways to share their wisdom with younger generations.[8]

Perhaps you question whether or not wisdom is a term which applies to you. "I'm not that old yet," you may be thinking. How should we define wisdom?

Some link wisdom to a high level of mental development or problem-solving capacity. Others think it has something to do with personality development. One recent study pointed to a combination of attributes like understanding, empathy, peacefulness, introspection, intuition, knowledge, and experience. Most people would agree that wisdom can come from long experience in living, although it isn't guaranteed.[9]

How does a wise person behave? People who are wise listen to others, know how to weigh evidence and how to offer advice. They have the skills needed to work with a variety of people and the ability to make good judgments. They have learned to profit from the knowledge and experience of others, to learn from their own mistakes, and to accept the imperfections of others.[10] Balance seems to be in evidence; balance of thought and action, of head and heart, of past and present.

Our problem with the concept of wisdom may be that we so often view it as a stagnant endpoint. We see a bearded old codger high on the mountain with the seekers of wisdom making a long trek for enlightenment. Instead, learn to see yourself in these descriptions and images in a very practical way, and you will find that grandparenting can be welcomed as an opportunity to apply and test the lessons you have learned. We're told that "love isn't love 'til you give it away." Wisdom, I think, must operate in the same pattern. Trust yourself enough to go into this new-fashioned role with confidence and the will to continue learning and growing, teaching and sharing.

CHAPTER 2. Finding Common Ground

Grandparenting is personal. It isn't really defined by one's generation or age cohort, although we are influenced, to some degree, by the ideas that permeate our society about this role. Grandparenting is a one-on-one experience. But is it as simple as arranging a monetary legacy, reading stories, going fishing together or any of the other things that have been described as doing what comes naturally?

As he was writing his views on grandparenting, which were published in 1981, Dr. Dodson did some informal research. He talked with a number of kids between six and fourteen and asked them what things they had been taught by their grandparents. Apparently, Dodson had some personal expectations about what he might hear, because he was very surprised and distressed to learn that most of the youngsters reported that they hadn't learned anything in particular.[1]

What Is the Point of Grandparenting?

One popular, current theme is that the very thing grandchildren most need from grandparents is unconditional love. For some that means pure love unfettered by demands or requirements. This approach is often put forward as a counterpoint to the role of parents who must perform as disciplinarians. But does this notion of unconditional love mean that grandparents should be somehow devoid of expectations about the behavior of their grandchildren? For many grandparents that is just what it means.

GRANDPARENTS AS ENTREPRENEURS

Stephen Covey, for example, who is widely known for his motivational work with adults, made his position clear in his recent book for families. Writing as a parent, he endorsed unconditional love as a prerequisite for all children, yet he carefully defined expectations for the family as a unit and for its individual members. In this interpretation, unconditional love does not preclude standards or expectations.[2]

The children who were interviewed in the mid-1970s study by Dr. Arthur Kornhaber and his colleagues revealed in their drawings and verbal descriptions that grandparents were people a kid could count on for time and attention. They were an essential part of a full and normal life. Everyone knew just what they looked like, too! Dr. Kornhaber summarized the research results and concluded that grandparents have several important roles: historian, transmitter of religious faith and values, mentor, role model, wizard, and nurturer.[3]

The information that was revealed in his research described a particular time and place, but it spoke from the hearts of children. What would a replica of that investigation uncover now, some 20 years later? A small clue is revealed in this title of a recent book, *Funny, But You Don't Look Like a Grandmother.* Even the kids seem a bit confused by the way things have changed.[4]

I believe that the definition of what is most fundamentally important should cut across age cohorts, personal style, and changes in the family structure. Everything else could be cast aside, if necessary, except for that basic element. How would you define the core of the grandparenting role? Ask yourself these questions: What is the essence of grandparenting? What is the purpose?

First, it seems to me that grandparenting should be less concerned with what the older generations can do or want to do, and that it should be more concerned with the question of what it is that children need. But even this question is too general because, of course, they need many things. A more fruitful approach could be to ask ourselves to define the results of good grandparenting.

What Are the Results That We Desire?

We have the capacity to comprehend the general stages of our grandchildren's lives. We know the importance of their formative years by reviewing our own lives. Since we intend to provide a positive influence on their development, we must ask ourselves what kind of people we want them to become as adults.

Don't you want the new generation in your family to be competent, caring, honorable, resourceful, able to make and keep commitments, dedicated, balanced in work and play, and to know right from wrong? If we remain true to our own beliefs and training, then we would want them to be recognized as fine, upstanding American men and women, as people of good character who are civil in their relationships, and who are good citizens.

If we were to agree that this general description would be our deepest wish for every grandchild, then we could turn to the second step and begin to formulate a shared definition of the nature of our grandparenting role. This goal would reveal our concern for and our dedication to the support and regeneration of our culture's highest standards, and it would focus our interest in basic American values.

In 1992, pediatrician T. Berry Brazelton, M.D., wrote, "The value systems that strong families pass on are important to individuals as well as to our society. Grandparents are the vital link in the continuity. Our culture in the U.S. has lost far too much of this continuity and we are paying a terrible price for it."[5] Shared standards and beliefs that are retained and passed down generation after generation produce a more stable society. When grandparents play a significant role in sharing knowledge and wisdom, we function as the cultural bridge which binds us together over time as one people and one society. We, the elders, know who we are, where we came from, and what we are about in this world. By actively and purposefully sharing our morals and values with our grandchildren, we can contribute to a general sense of certainty and stability throughout society.

As a society we are engaged in an intense debate, both in public and private, around the issue of fundamental values and the ways in which they should be expressed in our behavior. Much of the attention and concern is focused on children and their development. We find ourselves in a terrible predicament founded upon differences over the proper definition of values and their appropriate application in everyday life. How does a person of good character behave? What is the meaning of a civil society? What are our obligations to each other as citizens? These choices

GRANDPARENTS AS ENTREPRENEURS

and decisions seem to be made on the basis of immediate expediency rather than upon traditional standards. Our collective distress is set against a backdrop of destructive attitudes and behaviors that are evident at all levels of society. The results of these negative attitudes and behaviors affect our neighborhoods, our cities, our jobs, and our relationships, and they certainly influence our youngest people.

Whether or not you feel personally affected by the debate, there is no escaping the fact that our children and grandchildren are dealing with problems, temptations, threats, and dilemmas that most of us never had to confront. The specific issues range from cheating on tests, drug use, corporate stealing, and Internet pornography to a host of other situations both large and small.

If we decide that the most meaningful challenge for grandparents is to have a positive effect on the lives of our own grandchildren during their growth and development, then we need to look at the significant issues that will affect their lives. The circumstances of daily life point directly to the topics of American values, moral standards, and individual behavior choices, and this focus gives us the chance to create an exciting, meaningful role for ourselves as grandparents.

Why Should We Consider These Issues?

Think about the following questions. How do you plan to make good use of all the things that you have learned and experienced in your life? Have you ever felt that your hard-earned knowledge and skills are being wasted? What good is your expertise if you can't help someone by sharing what you know?

Our involvement in transmitting basic values, appropriate behavior standards, and life skills is imperative. Our society needs a strong stabilizing element. We, the elders have what it takes to make a substantial contribution. We will respond constructively. We can do these things because we have the knowledge; we have the strength and health; we have the time; and we have the will to see things through. Our collective role can be and should be one of leadership in renewing our cultural conscience.

Those of us in the middle-age range, from about 45 to 65 years, may be most likely to embrace a new-fashioned style of grandparenting,

Finding Common Ground

although no volunteer will be refused. Because of the particular circumstances in which we were raised, it is probable that the majority of us share a set of common values. We have similar expectations about standards of behavior and of what is right and wrong. As children and young adults we were all influenced by World War II and its aftermath.

Courage, duty, and honor are values that were entirely real during that time in American history. They were personalized through participation in activities like Scouting and service clubs. Personal commitment was acknowledged daily as we pledged allegiance to our country at school. As children, we bore the mantle of individual responsibility and, as a result, we developed high standards of personal accomplishment and integrity. Serious attention was focused on our school performance by parents, educators, and the community so that we would be equal to the demands of adulthood in a competitive and dangerous world. Academic excellence was the goal for every student.

Our country had an acknowledged enemy then and that enemy had the threat of a bomb to enforce an alien way of life. The words "duck and cover" had universal meaning for many of us as children. During World War II, the citizens of London, for example, practiced air raid drills by going to underground shelters; in our schools, we were taught to duck under our desks and to fold our arms over our heads. This drill made the threat more than an intellectual concept; it seemed entirely real to us. We absorbed the expectations that we would grow up and participate in helping to out-smart and out-maneuver our national opponent. We believed that it was our duty and responsibility to do so in order to preserve our way of life.

We gained an appreciation of our own neighborhoods and communities along with the belief that we should leave things that we all shared and enjoyed better than we found them. Mere respect was not enough; each of us had a personal responsibility to be actively involved in making improvements. This altruistic ideal represented a universal responsibility that was expected of us and is something that we still take seriously. It is exemplified by President Kennedy's familiar advice to ". . . ask not what your country can do for you—ask what you can do for your country." On a global scale, the Peace Corps was one mechanism for the expression of this ideal that was, and still is, embraced by many Americans.

GRANDPARENTS AS ENTREPRENEURS

In the decade following the Second World War, young Americans grew and matured in relative peace and safety, with a sense of optimism, in the midst of good manners, with knowledge of our interdependence, and with expectations of individual self-restraint. We absorbed a belief in hard work, and a natural habit of helping neighbors.

It should not be surprising to discover that many of us, after years of working, learning, and raising our own families, have begun to experience a fresh desire to give something back. Whether or not this is a function of middle age or a generational heritage hardly matters. We retain a persistent belief in personal accomplishment coupled with a strong sense of responsibility for others.

These observations come from my recollections of growing up during the 1940s and 1950s. Of course, many adults who experienced that period wouldn't particularly agree with this description. There were many social problems and difficulties. Still, family historian Stephanie Coontz has noted that the 1950s are consistently described as the best decade in recent memory for raising families in the United States. We have become downright nostalgic about that time period. Why? For one thing, as she notes in *The Way We Never Were,* real wages grew rapidly as economic recovery began to take hold after World War II. People returned to the needs of home and family. There were fewer and less complicated choices for kids and parents to deal with. Family structure was predictable with fewer marriages ending in divorce. People were protected from unpleasant news about social or family problems because there was little media coverage of these topics. A shared moral order which supported family life existed within communities, and there was a feeling of hope for the future.[6]

Many of us wish that we could be grandparents under such conditions, but we are not going to be. That doesn't mean that we can abandon the challenges of modern society.

If properly organized and focused, the values that we have held all of our lives can become powerful tools for grandparenting. Remember that it is people who change society, and ours won't improve unless and until we decide to make it better.[7]

CHAPTER 3. The Challenge

What are the distinguishing characteristics of our society at the close of this century that converge to produce a major challenge to the very nature and practice of grandparenting?

- Life spans have lengthened so much that older Americans have a variety of opinions on the meaning and purpose of the grandparenting role.
- Significant numbers of grandparents are no longer physically close enough to their grandchildren to be daily, living examples of maturity.
- There are few consistent role models to exemplify basic values and behaviors.
- Lifestyles and attitudes have changed so much that new parents are faced with an unfamiliar system of values.
- There is no longer a clear, unspoken consensus on shared values as there was at mid-century.

Fortunately grandparents remember times past when there was a greater degree of community conformity in expressing values based on a shared understanding of what was right and what was wrong. Whatever particular age cohort we represent as individuals, we can, as a group, make use of that experience as the foundation for present-day grandparenting.

What Is Missing?

A proposal that grandparents might consciously focus on imparting values in an organized way seems rather alien. All of our experience tells us that values are conveyed by example. In previous generations, grandparents demonstrated their values and beliefs in their daily lives, and children were there to observe and mimic them during the natural course of everyday activities. The behaviors that exemplified those underlying values were part of the reality that youngsters simply experienced and absorbed. As we all realize, this no longer describes the lifestyle of many, many American families and hasn't for several decades.

One thing we do know is that with regular contact between generations, there are opportunities for older family members to offer a wise

GRANDPARENTS AS ENTREPRENEURS

comment or simple bit of good advice to the youngsters. More than likely these interactions consist of impromptu comments made during a brief conversation, a lucky confluence of timing on the part of the adult and receptivity on the part of the young person. Nonetheless, those wise words can remain clear and influential from that day forward. It is this particular experience, which may be nothing more than a brief encounter that brings together a meeting of minds and hearts, that can give us direction in the development of a useful method for modern grandparenting.

My proposal, in a nutshell, is that this serendipitous moment of meaningful conversation be recognized and elevated to primary importance. For grandparenting purposes, however, the concept must be crafted and honed with all of the wisdom, skills, and expertise that mature adults can bring to the challenge of transmitting cultural values. I believe there is potential here for the creation of lifelong relationships, very special and personal relationships, between modern grandparents and their grandchildren.

Unfortunately, no one is asking grandparents to play a part in explaining good values and good behavior, and so we must take the initiative.

It is true that retirees are a potent political group when it comes to influencing government programs that affect our own lives. We can comprehend the promise of channeling the vast resource that grandparents represent. Many things seem possible through engaging that power and refocusing it towards the philosophy of giving back to society.

Consider the sentence, "It takes a village to raise a child." It means that shared community standards are vital, and that individuals outside the nuclear family should be reliable and relied upon when it comes to raising children.[1] Is anyone asking what grandparents can do other than baby-sit? To wait for an invitation is to assume defeat. The opportunity is evident and it is up to us to respond and to demonstrate our beliefs by our actions.

How Do We Proceed?

We have defined a worthy grandparenting goal; that is, the transmission of our cultural conscience—meaning the values and ideals that older Americans cherish, our history as a people, our belief in standards of character and civility, and our hopes for the future—through focused conversations. The next requirement is to develop a simple system that will help us to prepare for this challenge and to manage it effectively. Equally important is the capacity to replicate the results of using this strategy by appealing to grandparents across America to make a commitment and join in the process.

There is immense strength in our numbers and our distribution; we are everywhere at once. At the same time, each of us is an independent person and each of us acts within a small family structure where we serve as grandparents and/or stepgrandparents. There are fundamental beliefs that we all share even though we are all unique individuals. This means that we can act together independently. That's a powerful and promising idea!

I have emphasized group behaviors and attitudes based on age cohorts, but when we consider the reality of our grandparenting role, we must also acknowledge this truth: our role is performed by individuals and couples. If we want to change the definition of the role, we must look to individuals, ordinary people like you and me, to accept the challenge of participation and experimentation. This necessity for individual initiative calls to mind the spirit of the American entrepreneur.

How Can Grandparents Be Like Entrepreneurs?

Perhaps even more than the desire to have wealth or social status, Americans dream of being the boss and starting a business in order to do so. We pride ourselves on this independent, entrepreneurial spirit. Here then, is a new opportunity to cast yourself in just such a role.

Many of you will immediately think about the development of small, high-tech companies when the word entrepreneur is mentioned. Others might envision an inventor who is trying to solve a problem by devising something unique in the marketplace. The term entrepreneur suggests something exciting, daring, and original. An entrepreneur is a person who is driven to achieve something specific because she or he finds a deficiency or recognizes an unmet need and interprets this as a challenge and a call to action. Remember, where there's a will, there's a way.

An entrepreneur has the inner spirit and confidence to set off on a great adventure where the destination is only a dream in the mind's eye. This is true whether you are starting a high-cost computer business or exploring the mysteries of Malaysia looking for new plants that may yield

GRANDPARENTS AS ENTREPRENEURS

needed pharmaceuticals, or starting a whole new career at mid-life. Inevitably, such a person is enthusiastic, optimistic, and determined.

Although faced with problems and frustrations, the entrepreneur is neither deterred nor dissuaded from the task, but remains focused on the dream. No one starts a new business venture with the expectation of anything other than complete success.

The role of a full-fledged entrepreneur is a useful concept for the development of some productive ideas about grandparenting because it represents the sense of enthusiasm and the can-do optimism that will lead us to success in our new role.

Where Do I Fit in?

During the course of reading this book you will encounter six IMAGINE exercises. Each exercise is intended to let you explore and develop the material that you have just read. You are encouraged to transform the words into a vision that makes them personal for you. Each exercise will generate thoughts, memories, feelings, and ideas that you can make use of as you apply the material to your own grandparenting style.

Reading a book like this is a lot like going to school again. The text and the how-to information are provided. But ultimately, of course, nothing happens until you actively participate.

Following each exercise you will find a worksheet where you can jot down the things that you will want to remember and review later. By imagining and then recording your thoughts, you will begin to clarify and to organize your own version of new-fashioned grandparenting.

Start now with IMAGINE: Exercise Number One.

> IMAGINE
> Exercise
> Number One

The Entrepreneur

- Have you ever felt that your knowledge and skills are being wasted?

The Challenge

- What do your grandchildren need to learn about life?
- What valuable lessons can you teach your grandchildren?
- What are your feelings about being a grandparent?
- Which elements are satisfying and which are frustrating based on your experiences or the reports of your friends?
- As a creative innovator, a person who is thinking like an entrepreneur, how would you improve your role?
- Can you imagine a whole new way to share your wisdom with your grandchildren and relate to each other?
- If that happened, would you feel more satisfied and fulfilled?
- How might your grandchildren feel and how would they respond?

WORKSHEET for IMAGINE: Exercise Number One

First, make a list of some of the practical skills that you have taught (or hope to teach) each grandchild as a result of activities that you have shared (or plan to share). For example, baking cookies together. You might conclude that in using a recipe, your grandchild learns the importance of following directions step by step.

_____
_____
_____
_____
_____
_____
_____
_____

GRANDPARENTS AS ENTREPRENEURS

_____
_____
_____
_____
_____

Second, make a list of other practical skills that you believe are very important for your grandchild's successful development.

_____
_____
_____
_____
_____
_____
_____
_____

SUMMARY

In Part One, the stage has been set for a modern form of grandparenting that is concerned with our values and ideals as a society. By understanding that we young elders share common beliefs and standards, it will be possible to act together independently as we work to change society for the better.

The format for our new grandparenting activity will be based on focused and purposeful conversations that are designed and produced by individual grandparents using the techniques and methods employed by professional consultants. An open, entrepreneurial frame of mind will be

The Challenge

helpful as we move forward in the development of this unique and creative grandparenting program.

In Part Two, we will use the world of business as an analogy for the role of grandparenting. My purpose in using a business framework is to endorse an appropriate, professional stature for the knowledge and skills that we possess. To start things off, you will receive a symbolic franchise offer and learn the first element of a formal, first-of-its-kind job description for grandparenting.

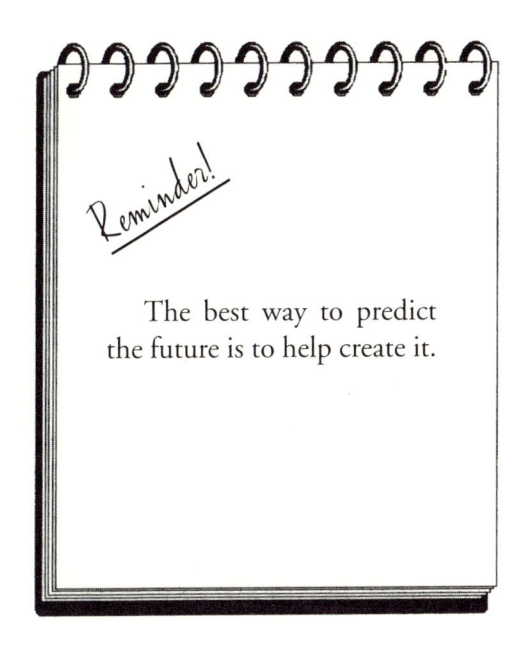

Reminder!

The best way to predict the future is to help create it.

PART TWO

A NEW JOB DESCRIPTION

What are the talents and skills that you might have to offer as someone who is contemplating an entrepreneurial excursion into independent consulting?

Review in your own mind the managerial skills that you have acquired from the many and varied activities and circumstances that you have experienced throughout your life. Some of your expertise may be the result of formal training, an MBA for example, or you may have encountered your learning opportunities while on the job. By themselves, parenting and household management require administrative skills such as coordinating and tracking the schedules of family members while organizing and timing healthy meals, homework, laundry, and so forth. Perhaps you have organized volunteer activities, served as a committee chair, or participated in political organizations or church activities.

These situations, and many more like them, have given you the foundation for modern grandparenting. I imagine that you have also refined your communication skills by working with a variety of people who have personality characteristics that are different from your own. Refining and enhancing our interactive skills is a natural outcome of having had numerous experiences in many different situations. By taking the time to review your life from the perspective of specific skills that you have

A NEW JOB DESCRIPTION

learned and perfected, you may be pleasantly surprised to discover just how accomplished you really are.

I would expect that the younger you are, regardless of gender, the more likely it is that you have received advanced education and perhaps even a graduate degree. Exposure to higher education inevitably increases our proficiency in many areas of life. According to U.S. census data, in 1940 women had a higher rate of high school graduation than men but a lower college graduation rate. However, at that time, only 4.6 percent of the total population had completed four or more years of college. Fifty years later, in 1990, the growing importance of higher education showed clearly in the census figures which revealed that 12.3 percent of the population had completed four or more years of college. Among men, 21 percent had earned a college degree and among women, 17 percent had finished at least four years of college.[1]

An interim census report on education revealed that by 1997 the proportion of young women who had completed four or more years of college again surpassed men in the same 25-29 age group, as they had in the previous year. These new figures showed that 29.3 percent of women and 26.3 percent of men had earned degrees. The old gap between the two categories had been closing since 1985, probably as a result of the growing importance of economic self-reliance among women. In the total 1997 population, men were still slightly ahead at 26 percent compared to 22 percent completion for women.[2]

With recent changes in the makeup of the American workforce, many women are, or have been, workers, managers, and business owners. This circumstance has, in turn, prompted a reorientation of home and family life. Both men and women are aware of the idea of marriage as an equal partnership without strict role definitions. The extent to which you have actually either initiated or responded to some of these changes in your own life will depend, in part, on the attitudes and the values of your own generation. Lifestyle changes which significantly alter our family roles and patterns also challenge us to develop skills that might not otherwise be required.

As parents, we were all influenced by trends that have gradually taken place throughout this century in the fields of human development and child psychology. Having experienced the rise and decline of numerous theories, we are inclined to be skeptical about expert advice and savvy enough to recognize "pop" psychology. Each of us tends to rely on the skills and precepts that characterized our own childhood although we are not adverse to searching for information from books on ways to improve ourselves or to get more out of life. For example, we are learning the details of investing in order to achieve better control of our financial futures. Many of us have become computer literate and comfortable with new modes of communication.

When we take all of these things into consideration, it is clearly reasonable and practical to apply the talents, skills, experiences, and expectations that we already have rather than to begin with something brand new; just as it would be futile to attempt to copy another culture's vision of grandparenting. And as individuals, each of us can retain a personal concept of what a grandparent does based on nostalgia, unique experiences, and our own family lifestyles, so long as we have a meeting of the minds concerning one vital aspect of the role.

Our consulting focus must be unified in the transference of our cultural values and ideals without any attempt to sacrifice individual personality. The development of a fresh consensus on a twenty-first-century definition of American grandparenting will give us the chance to turn our considerable resources and our individual accomplishments toward a universal task that is ours to embrace and perform.

CHAPTER 4. The Business Analogy

In many respects, business concepts and practices are incorporated into our everyday activities even if you've never quite thought of them that way. Of course, some of us will have had direct learning experiences through a family business, a spouse's company, a friend's business, or even our own enterprise. I feel comfortable in assuming that most of us have been employees at some period in our lives, and that alone has

A NEW JOB DESCRIPTION

given us an insider's view of a business operation. These examples are obvious, however, and I want you to realize that there are other, more subtle ways in which the business world is incorporated into our lives.

Just consider that running a household demands administrative skills and interpersonal skills, and that it benefits from planning, budgeting, research, comparative analysis, project management, and goal setting. Each of these elements is actually a routine household activity although we don't generally use these labels to identify them. In business applications each of these elements is distinct and is the focus of detailed evaluation. Therefore, a business model is replete with ideas and skills that can be borrowed and adapted for better grandparenting without really nudging our routine comfort zone. We can elect to transfer knowledge and skills between home and business uses at will.

Although it may still seem strange to equate grandparenting with the operation of a business, we now understand that an entrepreneurial analogy compels us to produce a model for implementation. A model is necessary if we intend to have a massive, national impact, and, in order to be useful, it must encapsulate a simple, productive, appealing activity that any adult can accept and put into practice. The first businesslike step was the identification of consulting as our model. This choice suited the needs of Dylan's grandmother, and we can be confident that it will come to benefit her client. Replication of a positive consulting outcome will require specific business skills and techniques that each of us must recognize and refine, or maybe even learn, to suit our grandparenting purpose.

If we can continue to see ourselves as entrepreneurs in this grand new endeavor, knowing that we intend to transmit out cultural values effectively by becoming expert consultants and project managers, then we can make use of other business methods as needed. By thinking like new business owners, we can be creative as we begin to design a workable yet still familiar framework for organizing our new-fashioned grandparenting profession.

In the future, grandparenting should be equated with a particular, distinct activity—a primary job responsibility—rather than being a title acquired by the birth of a new baby. In that future, every grandparent will have access to a job description and a training manual.

The Business Analogy

How Can We Use Business Ideas?

I grant you that in making use of business ideas, this grandparenting proposal is definitely unusual. It seems frankly odd at first. You may be inclined to wonder whether we should be looking at advice from educators and specialists in the field of child development. That would be the more normal course of events. We certainly won't neglect those elements, but we won't begin there. Just remember that entrepreneurs are known for crossing boundaries and doing the unexpected.

Think of the common phrases we use, such as "It's time to get down to business," when we want people to concentrate and produce. In this sense, business is relevant to our lives in general. If we accept the business world as a basic guide for our thinking about grandparenting, we can explore a ready-made system and that makes our task much easier because it's time for grandparents to get down to business.

Let's review some key points. A business of any type (commercial, industrial, or service) requires thought and planning. In this regard, we grandparents need to define and share a universal plan in order to work together independently. A business requires expertise of many types. We have certain kinds of solid expertise and yet we may need to review and update other skills. A business requires leadership. That's a position naturally assumed by the elders; however, we would do well to investigate modern leadership standards and techniques. A business should have a clear purpose and a known process. As functioning consultants we will need a firm, overall grasp of *The Birthday Program* including its philosophy and its ritual elements. A business system separates tasks and assigns them to different people so that everyone knows her or his particular responsibilities. A clear job description for new-fashioned grandparenting will illuminate this basic business element.

By choosing to use a business analogy we can bring a professional stature to the role of grandparenting, and we can reinforce the idea that wisdom and skills are necessary for excellence in our job performance.

Because I believe that there is value in our sharing a somewhat structured method for grandparenting when it comes to imparting our wisdom and teaching good values, this proposal may seem to be completely serious. But don't equate serious ideas with a directive to be somber and

A NEW JOB DESCRIPTION

dull. None of us wants anything of the sort. In and of itself, structure does nothing to negate the warm, familiar, and charming elements of grandparenting. It is simply a hidden foundation. After all, business consultants who work for remuneration are everyday people with normal lives!

How Can This Be Personal?

In the event that concepts from the business world represent your comfort zone, this unexpected application of your skills should be most rewarding. On the other hand, if this scenario is foreign to your experience, you need not be concerned about arcane jargon or obscure references. The ideas will be presented in the most clear and straightforward terms possible because I want you to be comfortable in your new position. We need to be calm and confident so that we can focus on the job at hand in order to maximize results for our clients. After all, the shareholders in my family corporation, and in yours, deserve the best of our talents and resources.

Of course, there is no intention here of reducing children to the equivalent of packaged goods in order to make this association with the world of business. Companies, whatever they make or do, are really all about people and organization and, because this is so, we can tap the realm of human resource development and other general business practices in order to add value to our vision of successful grandparenting.

The intent is to create and design something so simple that any grandparent anywhere can take on the entrepreneurial challenge and expect to operate a successful, small consulting "business."

The Business Analogy

> **Reminder!**
>
> No one is being urged to give up any of the old-fashioned ways of grandparenting. If you are involved in traditional activities, don't change! Merely add this new element to your repertoire in order to develop and expand your relationship with your grandchildren.
>
> On the other hand, if you have minimal, superficial contact with them, view this new idea as one small thing that you can do to make a big difference.

This very practical, businesslike approach to grandparenting has several objectives:

- the isolation of a basic grandparenting theme,
- orientation of diverse grandparenting expectations around this common theme,
- concentration of time and effort on a single annual event which develops this theme,
- repetition of the method over time for continuity during childhood and teen years,
- creation of a ritualized event marking annual growth transitions,

A NEW JOB DESCRIPTION

- development of a meaningful grandparenting job description,
- and perpetuation of a process that links generations and fulfills a timeless responsibility.

Let's move forward now so that we can begin to address our role and responsibilities more directly and in detail. Are you ready to get down to business? Good, because I'm going to make you an offer that you won't be able to resist.

CHAPTER 5. The Franchise Alternative

This new method of grandparenting that I am proposing is very similar to owning a business franchise. A franchise is an approved replica of an original business, and by definition, it gives us a way that we can work together and still be independent. When we think about a favorite store or restaurant that is part of a franchise system, then we also know what to expect from any location in that chain because they are all functioning in the same way. They share the same process and product or service. This is one of the benefits that comes with the selection of a franchise.

This new style of grandparenting relies upon our shared use of a common process, *The Birthday Program*. Also, we now expect to share certain business planning and management functions, although we have not yet reviewed this material in any detail.

It is readily apparent to any discerning grandparent, however, that our clients are as separate and unique as individual people can be. A franchise might then be viewed as a limitation to the expression of individuality. When we realize that children grow through a series of ages and stages which are generally similar, we recognize that we will be able to share a great deal of basic information. For this subject matter, we will turn to appropriate, contemporary experts.

What Does Being a Franchise Owner Require?

This particular franchise is being called "user-friendly" because as an individual and as a fully independent operator you will find it easy to adapt *The Birthday Program* to your own circumstances. I expect you will be pleased to know that there is no club to join. There are no dues to pay. No one is going to come from headquarters to check up on you because there is no such place. However, on a more fundamental level, be assured that there are no requirements pertaining to ethnicity, nationality, religion, or politics. You can be a fabulous grandparent if you happen to be physically handicapped or live far from your grandchildren. This is an all-inclusive business in which you and your family remain completely free and independent even though we will all be linked by sharing a business philosophy and process.

This grandparenting business will make you feel challenged to become better at quality grandparenting than you ever envisioned you might be! If that is something you truly want to do, know that an honorary franchise is always available.

Clarify your reactions now by using The Checklist for Entrepreneurial Readiness.

THE CHECKLIST FOR ENTREPRENEURIAL READINESS

__ I enjoy the "fun" part of grandparenting, but I want to do more.

__ I know that I have acquired lots of wisdom and skills from all of my experiences in life.

__ I'm excited about the idea of helping my grandchildren learn the really important lessons of life so that they will have good values as they grow.

__ I have what it takes to make a serious commitment to a better style of grandparenting and to follow through.

__ I am curious to discover just what this concept is all about and what it can mean for me.

A NEW JOB DESCRIPTION

Anyone who answered these questions affirmatively is hereby granted an honorary franchise in *The Business of Life*.

As the creator of this concept and the founding franchisor, I have selected this name—*The Business of Life*—for our enterprise. I chose this name because it conveys two meanings. First, it represents the essential function of grandparenting which is the transmission of our cultural conscience to each new generation. Second, it refers to an organized, businesslike process that modern grandparents can use to participate in this vital role.

In the United States, business is regarded as serious and substantive. If we insist that grandparenting must be viewed by society as a professional skill, then a business comparison announces our intention to be taken seriously. Therefore, as this grandparenting process is explored and expanded, I will continue to make use of a business analogy and a franchise system for describing our new role.

SUMMARY

In Part Two, we explored the use of a business framework as a guide for organizing a focused role for modern grandparenting. Of course, this has nothing to do with money or finances. We are strictly volunteers. But in order to be successful, we must be no less organized and dedicated than any other new business owner who wants to stay in business because *The Birthday Program* calls for staying power.

As a newcomer to this process, you have been offered the opportunity to become an entrepreneur and to open an honorary franchise in this new venture, *The Business of Life*.

If you have decided to give this idea a try, you should be eager to discover what is coming next in this proposal.

In Part Three, we will continue to tap the methods employed by an entrepreneur to evaluate a franchise offer. First, we will undertake a kind of market research that is appropriate for grandparenting. Is there a place for this business in our society? What are our reasonable chances of success? This exercise will put us squarely in the midst of our culture and all its strengths and weaknesses. Because we intend to do something meaningful and helpful for the next generation, we must face and understand the world our grandchildren inhabit. Great effort will be made to explore the primary values and beliefs that Americans hold dear and to consider the behaviors that exemplify those values.

A JOB DESCRIPTION FOR GRANDPARENTS (Part 1)

Previously a question was posed: If there is a job title—grandparent—then why is there no job description? A clear definition of the job is certainly one of the most common and expected elements of employment.

Now that each of us has volunteered to become the manager/operator of a grandparenting franchise, *The Business of Life*, it is essential that we clarify the requirements of this position. Therefore, the first element of our new job description is presented based on the material covered in this part.

This job description will be expanded upon by adding new sections after each element of the business plan is discussed, so that there can be little doubt concerning the practical application of the information.

JOB POSTING

Please be advised that the following employment opportunity is now available.

BUSINESS OF LIFE GRANDPARENT
EXECUTIVE PROFILE

The successful applicant will be self-motivated, enthusiastic, confident, and will possess an entrepreneurial spirit. The inner drive to accomplish long-term goals is imperative and the enjoyment of young children is essential. This mature adult will want to share the important lessons of life and help guide a new generation of American youngsters by interacting "one-on-one" with his or her own grandchildren.

(Additional elements of the job description will be posted following each section of this guidebook.)

PART THREE

MARKET RESEARCH

Often, first-time entrepreneurs, including franchise purchasers, have business goals but lack the understanding of how to make their dream a reality. What should be done first, second, and so on? They can turn to a large body of literature and professional advice. In our situation, despite the availability of many books on grandparenting, none has yet defined a primary focus or a program for action. Like neophyte business owners, we do not yet know how to transform our vision into a practical enterprise. Dreaming is easy, but if we want to reach our goal we must have a plan.

What is our first step? Even though we have confidence that, as the elders of American society, we possess valuable knowledge and time-tested skills that need to be shared, it remains our responsibility as potential *Business of Life* owners to determine the need for our services. We must briefly evaluate the circumstances that will make this grandparenting proposal viable.

The process used by an entrepreneur to evaluate the potential for a business concept is called market research. Informally it's known as doing your homework. In order to be successful, the owner must know the wants and needs of projected customers. In our situation, grandchildren are the targeted market segment for whom we plan to provide *Business of*

MARKET RESEARCH

Life consulting services. We will work with youngsters from the approximate ages of four through nineteen.

Relevant questions for our focused style of grandparenting, and therefore our market analysis, would be: can a need be demonstrated for the proposed program, what is the market demand for the service, and is there a competing service already in place.

Can we be confident that there is a need for a new-fashioned kind of grandparenting? I wouldn't be surprise to learn that you have strong feelings and opinions about our society and the circumstances in which our grandchildren are being raised. We have all formed impressions concerning the nature of American life as it exists near the close of the twentieth century. These impressions are formed in part by the media and in part by our own memories of growing up along with the current experiences of family members, friends, and neighbors.

If we choose to be responsive to our grandchildren's need for support in their development of good character traits, in lessons on civility, and a broad appreciation of what it means to be a citizen of our nation and the world, then we must acknowledge and attempt to understand the realities of their lives.

How Can We Organize This Inquiry?

There are two levels of investigation. One is the equivalent of a "big picture" or broad-scale view of major issues that affect the society at large. This is formally called macroanalysis. From this perspective we will review some of those factors that are beyond individual control such as the content of television programs and commercials, which are both current topics of national debate. Televised material is an example of a national issue that both reflects and influences our collective ideas about personal attitudes, preferences, and behaviors and, therefore, our standards and values. When evaluating concerns of this magnitude we are dealing with decisions that can be expected to influence the lives of all our grandchildren in some way.

Even the most fervent and dedicated activist will be challenged to produce a meaningful change in any pervasive trend at the macro-level. These then are the broad topics which have been disseminated throughout American culture and may even include global matters. In some way, these issues tend to affect nearly everyone and they are almost impossible to ignore.

At the other end of the scale is the second level of inquiry which is made up of those things that comprise everyday life. Just as a snapshot is the opposite of the big picture, this small-scale, or micro, analysis, in terms of grandparenting, looks at the day-to-day features of an individual child's life. It is more personal and can reflect considerable variation depending on local circumstances and family choices. At the micro level there is often the opportunity to moderate the effect of general social influences. Whether a child may or may not watch a television program, for example, can be regulated by concerned parents but the child's visit to a friend's house may undo that decision. Our high-tech communication capabilities mean that an individual's daily experiences are far from being independent of broad-scale, macro impact. For now, however, I will leave further microanalysis for development in Chapter 7.

Make this research exercise a personal exploration. Use the following subjects as a springboard for your own evaluation of the state of our nation.

CHAPTER 6. Macroanalysis—the Big Picture

We use the expression "looking at the big picture" when we want to refer to circumstances that are broad based, sometimes national or even global in scope, and likely to affect most people in some way. This is the realm of macroanalysis.

As we Americans move through a transition period from one century to another, it is inevitable that we, as a people, will review the past and speculate about the future. A great deal of our public debate, as we approach and cross the century mark, will focus on lessons learned and issues yet to be addressed. At this juncture we find ourselves engaged in a kind of national housecleaning. The older we are, the more capacity we have to relate national memories to our own actual experiences of life

MARKET RESEARCH

and, in turn, we wonder what kind of world our grandchildren will inhabit in the twenty-first century.

Your assignment is to evaluate the state of our society today. Some of the issues will be brought up in this chapter but the material won't be comprehensive; whole books are written about this topic. My purpose here is to recognize key social changes that will impact *The Birthday Program,* because grandparents and grandchildren will bring different sensibilities to the interaction. Grandmother is going to have difficulty counseling Dylan, just as you and I will be at loose ends in working with our own grandchildren, without some understanding of the true nature of our society and the kinds of changes that have occurred since we were children. There are some subtle and some glaring differences between their generation's worldview and ours.

Even though you and I may feel personally untouched and uninfluenced by these large-scale changes in social behavior, we can't afford to ignore them. Our grandchildren are growing up in a particular time period that we need to understand. Nor would it be prudent to assume that change is slowing or even likely to stop. Modern grandparenting means active duty in real time.

In a more simple world that some would call ideal, we Americans would find ourselves sharing a common set of performance standards for family and community life based on internalized principles and values. It would be easy to raise children because the family and society would function in mutually supportive ways. Grandparents would live close by and would exemplify the sort of lives that everyone ought to emulate. They would represent the achievement of those shared ideals.

In many cultures today, this description of society is appropriate. However, our own society is suffused with ideals and values that tend to work against this gentle, stable picture. In a sense we are often our own worst enemy because we thrive on individuality, change, innovation, and discovery. We strive to improve and to advance. In the bargain, we gain some things but we often lose others.

The following material will touch upon some of the major, contemporary matters that we discuss with spouses and in gatherings with friends, coworkers, golf partners, family members, and neighbors. These issues are brought home to us when we read newspapers and watch the evening news on television. We care about these things because we are all affected by them in some way.

Here's an example. Comparisons between lifestyles, values, and behavior standards at the beginning and end of this century demonstrate major changes. Older Americans know that the basic institutions of society have become less certain. The once-constant underpinnings of "family, school, and church" have shifted and changed. The core values espoused by these institutions, once apparently held in common, have given way to a maze of new configurations.

Your own sense of just how good or how bad things are right now depends to some degree on your age cohort and your own experiences while growing up. For example, what are some of the changes in child rearing methods and subsequently some of the changes in the early lives of youngsters since the beginning of the century?

Psychologist John B. Watson was very influential, especially in the 1920s. He believed that children were "clean slates" when they were born and every trait they developed was a result of learned behavior. He expressed his views in prolific advice on how to raise children. In the 1920s, Watson proposed that children be treated much like miniature adults. He believed this kind of experience would encourage the development of adult behavior. In this view, parents were advised to be objective and firm. Hugs and kisses were too indulgent and holding children on one's lap was frowned upon. It was permissible to kiss them once on the forehead when they said goodnight. Parents were encouraged to shake hands with them in the morning and to reward exceptionally good behavior with a pat on the head.[1]

In the context of Watson's recommendations, it may not be so difficult to comprehend why Dr. Spock was later accused of permissiveness in the child rearing advice he provided. And what about the world of older kids?

You probably know that the word *teenager* first came into popular use about the time of World War II. During the first half of this century, most kids in that age bracket had to work for a living. They had an immediate responsibility, a vital adult-like role that contributed to society, and in this context Dr. Watson's recommendations make more sense. Gradually, a series of social changes began to alter the nature of childhood and teen years: the prohibition of child labor, the growth of formal and

MARKET RESEARCH

extended schooling, technological developments, and the decline in the need for farm labor. Where teens were once introduced into the adult world through work, they were slowly separated from it and became characterized as students whose only job was to learn in a classroom.

With memories of earlier times in our heads, we must evaluate life as our grandchildren experience it now. In contrast to the first half of this century, teenagers can hardly expect to support themselves or a family without a high school education. Where it was once common for teens to learn on the job as they worked beside adults, now there is only one viable option for the majority. A high school degree is essential, but now a college degree is almost as necessary as a high school diploma used to be. College, however, is becoming more and more expensive and course work is not always immediately productive. Sometimes additional training is necessary to finally secure a good job. Meanwhile, very little is expected of teens for years and years other than to study and stay out of trouble. Some believe that this absence of a useful role in society (which meant productive, gainful work in the past) is the most common problem that teens share. We may be too superficial when we blame the entire youth "crisis" simply on a loss of morals.[2]

Until mid-century teenagers were viewed as immature and in need of adult guidance. They tended to act like young adults who wanted to emulate their elders.[3] A significant shift has taken place in that pattern. In the last fifty years there has been a steady transformation of teenagers into consumers. They have become a targeted marketing segment due to the new consumerism that flourished along with the prosperity that followed World War II, the rapid growth of television as an advertising medium, and the size and growing influence of the Baby Boomers. It didn't take long for the "teenage" phase of life to come into its own. Initially their independent behavior outraged adults but eventually this youthfulness was so pervasive that gradually adults began to envy and copy it.[4]

Today's teens have been molded into an independent age group characterized by its own attitudes and interests. This group is a dramatic force in the marketplace where teens are often regarded, or at least portrayed, as sophisticated rather than naïve. This is unfortunate in that parents, who may tend to view them this way, come to feel that they can spend

Macroanalysis—the Big Picture

less time parenting. It's easier for busy adults to ignore their needs.[5] Once this breech would have been filled by aunts and uncles and grandparents.

The experts on our changing society say that teen culture is not a mere by-product of our loss of values but was a direct outcome of prosperity, a new consumer society, and the age-graded and age-segregated educational system which strengthens teenagers' sense of peer group identity.

It is interesting to consider their problems from the perspective that teens lack a productive role in society. This is very similar to the circumstances in which we grandparents find ourselves and a condition which this book strives to rectify. Our common predicament should generate a sense of empathy and sensitivity on our part as we interact with our teenaged grandchildren.

Here is another cultural element to consider. Unfortunately, individuality, a value which is central to our way of life, seems to have been disengaged from our belief in community. Our commonalties are routinely ignored or discredited in favor of our idiosyncrasies and the specialized interests of ever-smaller groups. Our melting pot looks more like a stew. This makes it ever more problematic, as a nation, to define our shared goals. Individual "rights" so often appear to take precedence over personal restraint. Because individuality is often in conflict with what is best for the common good, our society suffers.

Other broad-scale changes that we are all aware of, or have personally experienced, involve the structure of the American family. Divorce and reconstituted stepfamilies are common. We regard dual-employed parents as the norm, but quality child care is a major issue. We worry about the social price that we are paying for many new lifestyle options. At the same time, we value the freedom of choice and lack of social censure that makes it possible for people to leave dangerous situations.

Against this social backdrop, we must deal with many new threats to our well-being. The horror of AIDS may seem remote or merely convenient to overlook but it knows no boundaries. The reality of STDs (sexually transmitted diseases) is everywhere. Drugs and their new designer variations are common though we grandparents may prefer to ignore such matters. Let's not forget alcohol and cigarettes, which are

MARKET RESEARCH

again popular with young people. Hand guns and assault weapons are on the streets, and even schools can't be assumed to be safe havens. In 1998 we witnessed school shootings by young children that were profoundly shocking. Today, school kids practice "stop and drop" routines. This is a very real survival technique but this time the enemy is "us."

There is environmental degradation, food contamination, and the threat of terrorism from without and within. We have even been warned about comets coming at us from outer space. This barrage of threats can be confusing. It sometimes leaves us, adults and children alike, feeling helpless.

When we make comparisons between early television programming and the proliferation of choices now at our fingertips, we know that television provides a large measure of entertainment in the form of violence, sleaze, and alternative lifestyles along with family programs that don't even seem familiar. Enter computers and the Internet along with debates about the V-chip and other methods of controlling children's access to adult material. This is not to completely disparage all programming or new technology which has improved our lives in many ways, but to recognize some of the unfortunate content that computer-literate youngsters can access. Mature adults make informed decisions about what to view and what to ignore. For our grandchildren, natural curiosity leads to exploration without restraint. The impact of adult themes comes at full force on impressionable young minds and hearts. What they see and hear is what they learn, and it represents life as they know it. They have no fallback position.

In our role as grandparents, we may choose to deny any of these items, to actively denounce them, or to take an intellectual stance on the basis that variations and choices enrich life. Nonetheless, they are part of the macro setting of American life and they do affect the developing sensibilities of our grandchildren and their outlook for the future.

I urge you to create you own "big picture" view of American life by thinking about and evaluating society and our major institutions. Compare this picture to your own memories and experiences. I would imagine that you and your spouse probably talk about these things, and more, over coffee and the newspaper or along with the evening news.

Make it a personal habit to counter the downside with an optimistic list of positive circumstances that can make the lives of your grandchildren better than your own.

For example, I would bet that if a computer is available to you, the simplicity and speed of E-mailing messages to your children and grandchildren is something that you really appreciate, especially since they are inclined to respond by using this technology. Are you sending photos as well as designing greeting cards on the Internet? Be sure to familiarize yourself with the kind of academic access available in their schools, and discover whether or not they are using home computers to complete some of their homework assignments. This new feature of our lives offers incredible resources and opportunities for everyone.

It would be simplistic to imply that all change is bad for that simply isn't so. It is more appropriate to recognize, as in the case of using the Internet, that there are both good and bad elements of most any example that we might discuss. I'm certainly not opposed to a sunny outlook! I don't care to be dragged down by pessimism any more than you do. I am concerned, however, about any tendency to ignore the negative aspects of life which can make our consulting approach superficial and less productive. It doesn't mean that we will force negative views on our grandchildren, but that we must be considerate and respectful of their real concerns and challenges.

In our grandparenting role, the question of how some of these large-scale trends affect individual attitudes and behavior.

What Macro-Level Behavioral Trends Do We Notice?
1. Language and Self-Expression

Those who came of age during mid-century will appreciate the following example. (Those of you who are younger will have to take this on faith.) You will remember a time in our society when swear words were not used in public. As youngsters, swearing was banned in our homes, at least within our hearing. Likewise, swearing was out of bounds in school and church. We weren't likely to find or read library books containing swear words back then. Of course, we weren't able to find basic information on the normal changes of puberty either, and that loss left us all rather desperate and prone to believe in rumors and tall tales. Ignorance is not always bliss.

MARKET RESEARCH

There were no swear words in the teen magazines we read nor were such words spoken on the radio or television. They were not part of movie scripts. In other words, nowhere in the daily routine of our lives did we regularly encounter the use of swear words. Contrast that with contemporary speech.

Eventually each of us perceived by some chance experience that there were some "adult" words which were "bad." When and if we experimented with their use in adult company, we were sharply reprimanded. I do remember substitutes though, don't you? Even some adults, in the throes of a powerful need to express themselves, would employ clever phrases that came perilously close to the real thing. That margin kept them decent while satisfying the urge. As we kids grew enough to begin to test the boundaries of adult prerogatives, we too created substitutes. My favorite memory is "baloney juice."

This is my recollection and it may not coincide precisely with yours. Your experience may not have been quite so squeaky clean, but I believe that we can agree on this point: swearing was reserved for adults (though not condoned) and the language spheres of adults and children were generally kept separate.

My purpose in focusing on vulgar words is to illustrate the nature of a social standard that was fundamentally and universally endorsed. Occasionally a transgressor would require correction, but the rule itself didn't get much attention. The prohibition against swear words was a cultural "norm" or unconscious standard. Norms make life easier because we don't have to think about everything we do and say. When everyone knows and acts on the rules out of habit, people experience less conflict, less misunderstanding, and less confusion.[6]

At a time within our experience, without any meetings or conscious mass consensus, there was a prohibition against swearing in polite company or the presence of children. It was beneath our collective dignity. There were simply "right" and "wrong" words and everybody knew the difference. And because these rules were so clear and so taken for granted by everyone, there was no need to conduct a special program to promote them. For the most part, children mimicked adults who followed the rule. Furthermore, it was such common knowledge that it was routinely enforced by everyone without need of debate, analysis, research, evaluation, or the attention of experts. It was just an accepted rule of behavior.

This remembrance describes a standard of belief and behavior that existed at the macro level of analysis in that it was almost universally shared in America, but it also reflected a micro-level reality in that it was practiced in many individual homes.

Use this example to think about other changes that have occurred in public behaviors that we now routinely accept. Do the members of your extended family discuss and debate social issues and behavior standards? Would you say that there is general agreement or dissention across the generations? Can you detect differences in behavior that reflect some of the macro-level trends?

2. A Matter of Character

Another major factor in our lives, once upon a time, was a sense of respect. Respect for people in positions of authority was shown by the adults we observed. It was the correct attitude for the property that we owned, that others owned, and it extended to public property as well. There was general respect for religion and tolerance of variations in its expression, and there was respect for our government and military. None of this could be equated with wholesale or blind approval. Of course there was debate and disagreement, but there was also consensus. Even an agreement to disagree was supported with respect, at least in public view.

Each war period, until Vietnam, gave us, as a people, a common focus and a common goal which unified us in many ways and which demanded sacrifices from most of us. During World War II, for example, even in our homes we felt the lack of many normal consumer products, but our deprivation was a kind of contribution. Even in the midst of hardship, respectful considerate behavior was exemplified for us and expected of us. It, too, represented a definite cultural norm.

There were rather precise expectations of our behavior at our every turn. This was a time, remember, when chewing gum in school was an infraction and spray painting graffiti was unheard of.

This former lifestyle, which no single organization planned or controlled, had successes and it had failures. There were limitations as well as benefits. Now, we feel nostalgia for its traditions and for the moral limitations that produced a more ordered and safer lifestyle for almost everyone.

3. Past, Present, and Future

These simple examples, the absence of swear words in society and of gum chewing in school, exemplified restraint and respect. While the examples are simple, the values underlying them are not. There is now some degree of distress surrounding the certainty that things *have* changed, for these old standards have all but disappeared. Consequently, as a nation, we are engaged in a discussion of values. This topic bears the brunt of our dissatisfactions. It also represents our hopes for a renewal of the redeeming features of times past. Would you mind living in a world with more respect and less foul language?

As we remember the past and attempt to analyze the influences that affect our grandchildren, we grandparents should give some very conscious and thoughtful attention to a whole range of other values and character traits which we endorse, and which we may simply assume are being absorbed by our grandchildren because that is the way it happened for us. As grandparents, our expectations for our grandchildren are based on a myriad of such values which we believe to be cultural norms. But are they?

Consider this new trend, which has been described in various media reports, and is loosely called the "cult of the child." In this version of child rearing, parents do not tolerate any denial of their child's desires. Neither the school, the community, nor people in positions of authority have any right whatsoever to impose rules, restrictions, or limitations on the rights of their children. Some versions of "pop" culture and "pop" psychology may have converged to produce this horrifying vision of children in charge and of parents who promote this attitude. These kids are not expected to recognize limits nor to develop self-restraint. How do you feel about this arrangement in light of your own upbringing?

Our entrepreneurial challenge as analysts of the "big picture" is to remain informed about social events and debates, to be in touch with the real world as it exists, and to develop the individual capacity to translate this evolving social reality into meaningful content for our grandchildren. Our only hope for success is to deal with the development of character, civility, and citizenship in the circumstances that affect their lives here and now. This will not be simple nor will it be easy. It is a real job and it represents a definite shift in the concept of grandparenting.

CHAPTER 7. Microanalysis—the Local Snapshot

In contrast to the big picture perspective, a local snapshot helps us focus on smaller pieces of geography where our grandchildren live and where decision making and the consequences are close to home. This is the realm of microanalysis. Good grandparenting means taking both camera positions into account.

Ask yourself this question: Are your grandchildren absorbing a common, clear set of fundamental values in their own daily lives? This question leads us to a level of market research where you must do your own assessment of the circumstances. While it is critical that each entrepreneur consider the national scope of the debate over values, the only opportunity most of us have to deal with the situation is within our own families. While national solutions may be proposed for large-scale impact, the real work gets done one-on-one, person-to-person.

The essential issues of life are faced every day by individuals and our values are expressed by the decisions we make about our lives and our relationships. We are confronted regularly with decisions and choices. Often we face the dilemma of "choosing between an act of convenience and an act of conscience,"[1] according to Dr. Laura Schlessinger. It is our response to these choices that defines our character. Learning about this dichotomy between convenience and conscience is basic.

People aren't born with either a strong or weak character. We achieve strength of character by a long process of learning. The definitions of right and wrong are absorbed first from family and then from all of life's experiences beyond family relationships. Initially, we watch, listen, and mimic. We need encouragement and support to practice, make mistakes, and try again. Gradually, we have to learn to do the right thing when no one is watching to praise or reward us afterwards. We incorporate the rules and make them our own. The more cohesive the society over long periods of time, the easier it is for individuals to make this transition to mature character development.

In America, there is evidence, as we have seen in our brief exercise in macroanalysis, that our society would benefit from a renewal of the now "old-fashioned" traits that form the basis of good character. We savor our

MARKET RESEARCH

rights to choose, but we seem to need more lessons in making good choices. Our grandchildren need to know right from wrong. They need to learn more about the reciprocity of relationships, of what is legitimate to expect of others, and what we must offer in the bargain.

Too many of us have become self-indulgent, self-centered, and in need of constant pampering. Young people too often require that others supply whatever they want or need, and they seem to believe that the "right" partner will make them happy at all times. A recognition of the need for self-reliance and personal responsibility is in order. We need to talk about how civility works and why we should personally invest an effort in doing our part and doing it consistently. True citizenship can only exist when character and civility are embraced, practiced, and taken for granted.

The *Business of Life* describes our intention to share these basic things that we adults have learned and to focus on value clarification in the real world which our grandchildren inhabit. As an entrepreneur you must give some critical thought to evaluating the circumstances of your own grandchild's daily environment.

What Is My Micro Assignment?

Please consider yourself a business investigator and treat this question as a very real market research assignment.

If you are close enough to be knowledgeable about the regular activities and the lifestyle of your grandchild, you will already have either a sense of satisfaction or concern about his or her life and perhaps some of both. In the event that you and your offspring live in distant places your knowledge is likely to be incomplete. Some things which everyone might consider in evaluating a grandchild's situation would include the following topics: Are there strict or lax behavior standards at home and at school or daycare? Is there a presence or absence of an active religious foundation in the child's life? Is television usage monitored in any way? What kind of music does he or she favor? Does the child have ready access to a computer and the Internet? What kind of extracurricular activities are present on a regular basis, such as sports or music lessons? Is there a family pet to be cared for on a regular basis? Is each child expected to do chores? Is the child expected to dress himself, fix school lunches,

Microanalysis—the Local Snapshot

clear the table, wash or dry dishes, and so on? Is he or she expected to pick up toys or take care of his or her bicycle? How would you evaluate the neighborhood and community settings?

The idea behind asking yourself these questions is to acquire some sense of the regular influences on your grandchild's life so that you can form some basic assumptions about the kinds of values he or she is learning. You will need to form a kind of background picture of the child's reality. Even if you live close by, it would still be advisable to pay some attention to this assignment. Taking notes can be useful for later reference. Be assured that Dylan's life is carefully observed by Grandmother's eagle eye or listening ears. She realized early on that it was necessary to keep an individual file for each grandchild and she would undoubtedly recommend the same to you. She uses her notes to develop lines of inquiry for future consultations.

Can We Really Make a Difference?

Did you find your market research assignments interesting? I hope that you came up with independent issues and questions of your own. If you are a willing, intrigued, and enthusiastic entrepreneur, you will want to continue this opportunity to learn and to grow into a new grandparenting job assignment.

Take this opportunity to experiment with IMAGINE: Exercise Number Two.

**IMAGINE:
Exercise
Number Two**

The Slingshot

- Picture yourself outdoors on a marvelous day.
- You're wearing your favorite pair of jeans and you have pushed an old slingshot into your hip pocket.
- Walk through a field towards a stately oak tree.

MARKET RESEARCH

- As you meander, remember your childhood, think about your experiences, examine your convictions.
- Think about the beliefs that make you the person you are today.
- Take out the slingshot and pack those thoughts into the strap.
- Pull back and sling them out, away from you, and into the future. That's where they belong.
- Your grandchildren will need them out there.

WORKSHEET for IMAGINE: Exercise Number Two

First, make a list of those character traits that best describe the person you have become. Put a star next to the one positive characteristic that you believe has been the most important of them all.

_____

_____

_____

_____

_____

_____

Second, put down the name of each grandchild who is at least four years old. Now record three character traits for each child, positive things that you see them struggling to understand and to practice. Plan to help reinforce their efforts. (If you haven't been able to observe their behavior recently, make a phone call for information about their current activities from which you might draw some conclusions.)

_____

_____

Microanalysis—the Local Snapshot

It is inevitable that each of us will compare our own experiences as children and teens to the unique and particular circumstances that young people now experience. We must reconcile our memories and beliefs with the basic realities of life today. In order to be successful, our values and standards must be transformed into practical, useful guidance that is age appropriate.

Grandparents can't and shouldn't try to assume the sole burden as change agents in the quest for values clarification and for the extra training that children now need. However, grandparents must become full managing partners in the substantive fundamentals of life.

Nothing in this proposal will suggest that under normal circumstances we should see ourselves as substitute parents. Our adult children deserve our respect and support as they assume the full responsibilities of parenting. The point of *The Business of Life* is to refocus and promote grandparents as wise elders who are smart enough to be contemporary and skilled enough to become involved.

Are We Dealing wth a Viable Business Proposal?

The underlying theme of market research is to help us determine whether we have identified a legitimate need and, if so, to examine the extent of demand for the services we intend to supply.

You and I know that there are other, very serious efforts being made in this country to address the issue of our values. School personnel, churches, authors, child development specialists, and politicians speak to this issue. It may actually be difficult to identify a known group that does

MARKET RESEARCH

not, or has not, had something to say recently about the state of American values. The extent of the dialogue and the controversy demonstrates a keen awareness of our distress.

In *The Business of Life,* the presence of these competitors does not diminish the potential for a new version of grandparenting because all of these efforts are mutually supportive. The more participation, the more likely it becomes that we will arrive at a truer representation of community consensus. We may conclude, then, that this business proposal is valid and viable, and it is completely natural to expect that society's elders will have a role to play in the arena of American values.

What Advantage Does This Business Venture Have over the Competition?

Our best advantage is our distribution. There are potential franchise operations anywhere there are grandparents or grandchildren. We can act together by sharing a common process, yet we can do so independently. This is a major asset.

Our second advantage might appear to conflict with traditional grandparenting. However, this conclusion is incorrect. While *The Business of Life* does not deny or diminish any other style or component of grandparenting, it does endorse a focused effort. Every *Business of Life* entrepreneur signs on to the development of a conscious process of grandparenting. It is a substitution for a lifestyle that is fading away. This new concept is a direct attempt to establish a senior-adult role through a meaningful process that will influence future generations.

Our third advantage lies in the franchise system itself. The mere presence of a formal system with a definite procedure helps to relieve the pressure of trying to deal—alone—with the application of these ideas. It is the comfort that a franchise provides in the assurance that others are working close by on the same process.

One thing is certain. There is no competitive proposal which has such broad-based scope or a more natural group of practitioners. All in all, there seems to be little downside risk and plenty of upside potential.

If the concept has merit, it will become routine and then eventually recognized as a function of grandparenting. It will be retained, as a model, if our customers find value in *The Birthday Program*—so much so that they, in turn, become *Business of Life* grandparents.

Our own macro- and microanalysis of social circumstances reminds us of the breadth and depth of the grandparenting challenge. We will want and need to communicate with each other to compare and share experiences. (See the Author's Invitation in the back of this book.)

SUMMARY

In Part Three, we reviewed the background information grandparents need for this project. General social circumstances were touched on and the individual circumstances of each child's daily life were considered. Plenty of room was left for every franchise owner to explore and to personalize his or her own picture of modern reality.

Next, in Part Four, the spotlight will be on values.

A JOB DESCRIPTION FOR GRANDPARENTS (Part 2)

There is a false impression that older adults want to withdraw from intense involvement with young people. The truth is that most of us are still very much involved in everyday life. We may be raising our youngest children, are likely to be employed, and may also be dealing with the demands of our own elderly parents. Many of us have retired, but are still actively involved with family members, church affairs, political affiliations, recreational and cultural activities, and community organizations and activities. Many of us volunteer our time and skills to help local service organizations. We read newspapers and watch the evening news. We talk with friends and neighbors.

Most of us are completely aware that numerous changes have occurred in our society since we were young, and we want to help our grandchildren deal with the realities of life.

The next element of our new job description incorporates the material found in Part Three. The complete description will appear following Part Nine.

MARKET RESEARCH

> **Business of Life Grandparent (Part 2)**
> **JOB CONTENT**
>
> Active research and information gathering will support professional results. Awareness of social issues and the daily environment of each grandchild forms the background for skillful consulting.

(To be continued.)

PART FOUR

VALUES AND BEHAVIORS

Where do our values come from? According to McKay and Fanning, authors of *Self-Esteem*, our beliefs are formed in response to basic human needs. From the beginning, human infants are dependent and so we need the care and approval of our parents to survive. Gradually, we begin to adopt their beliefs and standards so that they will continue to care for us. We learn not only about their view of things like working, patriotism, and the correct goals in life, but we also learn about attitudes, behaviors, and expectations. We follow their lead in the meaning of friendship, what a marriage is supposed to be and how it works (or doesn't), how to handle anger or pain, how to handle sexuality, how to treat relatives, whether or not we can show fear or uncertainty, and how responsible and self-sufficient a person should be.

Many of things we learned and absorbed from them about how to conduct ourselves were values that were more or less shared by others in society. As we have seen, however, even when it comes to a topic like grandparenting, social consensus changes over time so that people of different generations acquire dissimilar ideas about roles, behavior standards, and values.

Our belief systems aren't limited to parental influence, of course, and as growing children we soon encounter other youngsters. Once again, in our desire to belong to a group outside the family, we try to accommodate the expectations of our peers. We learn how to behave in handling our friendly emotions, our aggressive feelings, and what this group of people expects of us.

McKay and Fanning describe the third major force in the creation of a belief system as the development by each of us of a continuing need for emotional and physical well-being. Here they include the quest for self-esteem and the need for pleasure, excitement, and meaning in life. Our values are generated by parental, peer, and cultural expectations, and we feel the urge to accept these definitions because we need to be accepted and to belong as well as to feel good about ourselves.[1]

There are many sources of information about particular American values. Quite a few books have been produced in recent years in response to rapid cultural changes and new attitudes that seem foreign to many older Americans. Values and beliefs are in a state of fluctuation that frequently leaves already mature adults frustrated, annoyed, and sometimes even frightened.

In order to converse comfortably with our grandchildren and to act in concert as grandparents, we must first review the broad-based, general values that characterize this society. Then, in order to both appreciate and evaluate the habits, opinions, attitudes, and behaviors that our grandchildren exhibit and to provide them with guidance, we will make use of a simple value system that is based on what I call *"The Three C's."* "*The Three C's*" stand for Character, Civility, and Citizenship.

CHAPTER 8. Values Orientation

One way that children begin to perceive the presence of values that represent all of us is through the celebration of holidays. Fourth of July fireworks grab attention. Kids delight in the joy and the ritual elements of special holidays as each arrives during the year. Itemize our official holidays and you will have a good collection of some of the

Values Orientation

major ideas that we value. There are the contribution of early presidents, a remembrance of the war between the states, civil rights, religious events, veterans, the will to work, thanksgiving for our very survival in a new land, the birth of our country, and our Declaration of Independence. Our national story is retold through these annual observations, and the remembrance of these events is accompanied by celebrations.

Youngsters are often involved in various elements of the celebrations such as food preparation, clothing and costumes, music, and special activities that reinforce the experience, but the lessons should be deeper in content and should involve recognition of the basic things we cherish. Holidays give grandparents a shared point of reference with grandchildren and a chance to think and talk about our most cherished values. The older the child, the more depth of content you can find in these events.

A CONVERSATION

Setting: A home somewhere in America where the breakfast table is littered with sections of the newspaper along with two mugs of coffee. It is Sunday morning, the fifth of July.

Participants: Grandmother and Grandfather.

The occasion: A routine event that often includes spirited conversations.

The following topic has been prompted by a color photo in the newspaper that depicts a fireworks display and a young boy dressed in a Revolutionary War costume.

Grandmother: "Look, Honey, isn't this a terrific photo? The caption says that the Fourth of July event included kids riding their bikes which they had decorated. Isn't that great? I remember doing that. It makes a kid feel involved, you know? I'm glad to see this because I'm working on some background ideas for a chat with Dylan."

Grandfather: "Ahh, now I know why you were looking at those history books from the kids' section yesterday at the bookstore. What are you trying to do?"

Grandmother: "Well, I'm trying to get at the topic of citizenship. It's more difficult than character and civility. It occurred to me that with *The Birthday Program* focused on the grandchild's birthday, it would be smart to relate that to our country's birthday. What do you think?"

Grandfather: "Hmmm, citizenship can be a tough topic. You've got knowledge and then you've got participation. You've also got to think about how kids learn. Some are visually oriented, some learn by listening, and others are 'hands-on' people. I'd say you have to make it vivid and real."

Grandmother: "You mean stay away from intellectual concepts. But it depends on how old the kid is, don't you think?"

Grandfather: "Sure, but the topic still has to be practical and useful to them, otherwise you'll lose their attention. Learning sticks when it's reinforced by an activity."

Grandmother: "Okay, you're making some good points, and it looks like I've got to do a little more research and some more thinking before I'll be ready on this one."

To be honest, the conversation didn't end here. However, we can review this sequence for some valuable reminders.

1. Planning prior to a consultation with your grandchild will always make the outcome better.
2. Research can help you organize and clarify your thinking. Grandmother looked at two children's books to double-check her own knowledge of the Revolutionary War period, the dates, and the events surrounding the signing of the Declaration of Independence. Her next step would be to select a few highlights and create sample questions based on the age of the grandchild who will be involved. Grandfather would expand the discussion with participation in local activities like the Fourth of July parade, helping display the flag on the front porch, and decorating bike wheels or the dinner table. He wants us to be sure we combine what we do and why we do it when it comes to national holidays.
3. As Grandfather suggested, it helps a great deal to appreciate the growth and development stages of childhood. And by recognizing that there are different learning styles, you can shift gears when you realize that a point you are trying to make isn't getting across. Each of

Values Orientation

us must stay mentally flexible in order to redirect the conversation and recapture the child's attention when that becomes necessary. (These topics will be discussed in future chapters.)

Grandmother decided that her conversation with eight-year-old Dylan would include a math problem, "How old is our country right now?" First we need to know when our country was born. Then we need to know how old our country was on its last birthday. How can we use these numbers to figure it out?

4. Make notes of your ideas and jot down sample questions. Try hard to make "word pictures" so that young people can "see" what you mean. For example, you might ask how the delegates traveled from their homes to Philadelphia, the city where they ratified the Declaration of Independence. The answer, of course, is by horseback (or horse-drawn carriage) which is a much different picture from modern transportation. With older children you can get more involved with abstract concepts, but don't forget Grandfather's advice to make it real.
5. Consider using the Fourth of July as a topic no matter when your grandchild's birthday takes place. It is a wonderful focus for citizenship, and for understanding our national origins and our ideals.

In addition to shared, national holidays, there are many regional or local events that reflect and honor our diversity. They focus on some of the unique differences which are remembered but which we have been willing to temper in the interests of our daily lives in a blended society. The values and opportunities of American society are such compelling incentives that they have attracted immigrants from all over the world for all of our history.

Our religious origins came from a Judeo/Christian heritage, but we freely allow other religious beliefs to be expressed here. The Ten Commandments have long informed many of our behavior prohibitions or those things that "thou shalt not do." Nonetheless, the country was founded on the separation of church and state and we place a high value on this principle. At the same time, we must remember that the founders of our country based our form of government, when it was new, on the idea that religious belief was an important foundation for good decision

VALUES AND BEHAVIORS

making. "As John Adams said, in his first year as our first vice president, 'Our constitution was made only for a moral and a religious people. It is wholly inadequate to the government of any other.'"[1]

The Puritans, who came here from England to settle in a strange new land, are generally recognized as having set the standard for hard work, saving, regular habits, diligence, self-control, and sobriety. Our culture has been deeply influenced by these values.[2] Even now these beliefs represent our work ethic.

Other long-standing American values place an emphasis on achievement and success especially through individual effort whereas some other cultures endorse cooperation. Indeed, a common belief among Americans is that anyone who works hard enough can succeed in whatever he or she sets out to do.[3]

We are a people who find value in work. We speak of housework, yardwork, and schoolwork. We work for a living and value results and monetary compensation, but that's not all. We believe that an adult's sense of self-respect is dependent upon the work that the individual performs. Many of us feel aimless and lost when we retire because we feel that we have lost our place and our value in this society. Conversely, we do not value leisure and laziness is frowned upon.[4]

We like action and progress. We set out to shape and control our own lives. It isn't surprising that we also value efficiency and practicality. We look for mechanisms that will help us find solutions and for methods that will enable us to complete our tasks expeditiously. We apply rational thinking and scientific standards to our tasks.[5]

We also, of course, have a shared foundation in terms of social and political values. Our basic, fundamental value is political freedom. It is the basis for our free enterprise system and our way of life. As stated in the Bill of Rights, which are the first ten amendments to the Constitution, our way of life includes freedom of religion, of speech and of the press, the right to assemble peacefully, and to petition the government to change or repeal a law that denies citizens' rights. We are also guaranteed that our homes will not be searched without a warrant. We have the right to bear arms to protect ourselves, the right to a fair trial if we are accused of a crime, the right to be represented by a lawyer, and the assurance that we won't be retried for the same offense. Also, no one can be compelled to testify against himself. Rights that are not specifically mentioned are not taken away by their omission and powers not given to the government or prohibited by the Constitution belong to the States or to the people. Subsequent amendments ended slavery and ensured voting rights regardless of race or gender.

These rights give us the basis for equal treatment under the law of the land, and we place great value on the ideal of equality. But the result of social and economic freedom means that there will be inequality. As individuals, some of us become wealthy, many more of us do not, and some are poor. Therefore, we make a distinction between equality of opportunity and equality in the results. Our humanitarian values become evident as we try to mitigate the inevitable disparity in results.[6]

Some of the personal characteristics that we accept in conjunction with these fundamental values include honesty, frankness, optimism, and pragmatism.[7]

This emphasis on American values is fundamental to *The Birthday Program* and is not just an intellectual exercise. We must become adept at working comfortably with values and to recognize their presence or absence in the ordinary activities of our grandchildren.

Our next step is to move from concepts to real, daily activities and the personal behaviors that represent good values. (Grandfather would approve. It's time to "get real.")

CHAPTER 9. *The Three C's*: A Simple System for Grouping Values

The personal values that lend themselves to grandparent/grandchild interactions have been organized into three primary value clusters that encompass the core of any personal value system. The shorthand reference is *The Three C's*. They are surely as fundamental, as important, and as vital as "The Three R's."

VALUES AND BEHAVIORS

The Three C's **stand for the following:**

CHARACTER is the first *"C."*

Character represents the internal beliefs that a person holds, within a particular cultural system, which motivate the attitudes and behaviors of that individual. A person of good character behaves so as to exemplify the highest level of standards and values held by his or her society.

CIVILITY is the second *"C."*

Civility in one's interactions with other individuals implies a level of respect and decency that is characterized by the Golden Rule. It means that one knows and uses the rules and standards for proper interpersonal behavior in all circumstances.

CITIZENSHIP is the third *"C."*

Citizenship covers both the attitudes and behavior one exhibits in relationships and duties beyond the family such as respecting the property of others, courtesy to strangers, caring for the needy in some way, voting for and participating in local government, stewardship of the earth, and so forth. Citizenship encompasses our neighborhoods and communities, our country and the world.

With these three concepts in mind, *The Three C's* or *character, civility, and citizenship*, we can organize our thinking and our grandparenting program. But how do any of us recognize a value when we see one?

It may be easier to think of an adult that you admire and to think about the values this person must hold because you can recognize them through her or his behavior, activities, and words. Your description of this person would probably include terms that have meaning for adults, such as dedicated or honorable. Grownups assign specific values, by name, to the behavior choices that we observe in other people. Therefore, it might be said that words and behaviors reveal personal values in action.

Where do the behaviors that we admire originate? They are the outcome of a long learning process. Children are not born knowing what the adult concepts mean. Indeed, it takes some years of growth and development before they can manage abstract thinking. In order to convey the

The Three C's: A Simple System for Grouping Values

meaning of values to children, adults use descriptions of the way in which we want them to behave in certain circumstances.

By using the *Three C* value clusters, we can review both the adult definitions of various values and some of the behaviors that would exemplify those values.

Each of the following *Three C* categories contains a list of values which form the foundations for our American ideals. The definitions are presented here in standard textbook style and are expressed in adult terms. The value lists are then followed by a short section where positive personality traits are identified which represent many of those values, and a second listing shows us some of the measures of conscience and self-control which support those behaviors. Often it is the things we refrain from doing that represent the presence of a positive value.

I. CHARACTER

A. The following values highlight elements of good character as expressed in adult terms.

- Honesty: Being truthful and also not cheating, stealing, or taking unfair advantage.
- Faithfulness: A steadfast allegiance to a person, a cause, or an ideal.
- Trustworthiness: Behaving in a dependable and responsible way. You can believe that this person will act as she or he says.
- Responsibility: The ability to behave properly and to make the right decisions without needing to be watched or directed by someone else.
- Perseverance: If you do something with perseverance, you keep trying to do it and you do not give up, even though it is very difficult.
- Courage: A quality of mind that enables one to face danger in spite of doubt or fear. Also, to have the courage of your convictions is to have the confidence and strength of mind to do what you believe is right, even though other people may not agree with you.

VALUES AND BEHAVIORS

- Loyalty: Retaining faithfulness and allegiance to country, family, friend, cause, or duty.
- Duty: Doing something that you feel you ought to do because it is right or because it is part of a code of behavior that you believe in. Also, all the work that you have to do because it is part of your job or your position in society.
- Integrity: Strict adherence to a good and virtuous code of conduct.

B. This category shows some of the personality traits that reveal good character.

1. Positive characteristics are behaviors and attitudes that we like to see.
   - Persistence
   - Thoughtfulness
   - Dedication
   - Patience
   - High standards
   - Bravery
   - Independence
   - Industriousness
   - Motivation
   - Exercise of good judgment
   - Commitment
   - Confidence
   - Conscientiousness

2. These measures of conscience and self-control support the positive behavior choices.
   - Refrains from lying, cheating, or stealing
   - Practices obedience
   - Organizes time and possessions
   - Practices being neat
   - Sets goals
   - Resists harmful temptations
   - Practices punctuality
   - Delays gratification

II. CIVILITY

A. The following values show examples of civility as expressed in adult terms.

- The Golden Rule: Do unto others as you would have them do unto you.
- Respect: To feel and show deference, esteem, and consideration for others.
- Tolerance: Allowing other people to have their own attitudes or beliefs or to behave in a particular way even if you do not agree or approve.

The Three C's: A Simple System for Grouping Values

- Empathy: The ability to share another person's feelings and emotions as if they were your own.

B. This category shows some of the personality traits that reveal civility.
  1. Positive characteristics are behaviors and attitudes that we appreciate.
     - Politeness   • Courtesy   • Patience
     - Altruism   • Kindness   • Helpfulness
     - Tolerance   • Friendliness   • Thoughtfulness
  2. These measures of conscience and self-control are in support of civil behavior.
     - Taking turns   • Cooperating   • Sharing
     - Considering others   • Using good manners
     - Thinking before speaking
     - Being courteous   • Being open-minded
     - Avoiding foul language

III. CITIZENSHIP

A. The following values represent citizenship as expressed in adult terms.
- Freedom: The right to express views and opinions and to live or act within the law without the government interfering.
- Justice: Fairness in the way people are treated or the system that a country uses in order to make sure that people obey the laws and that punishment is given to people who break the laws.
- Nationality: The status, rights, and responsibilities that you have because of belonging to a particular nation.
- Equality: The same status, rights, and responsibilities for all the members of a group or a society.
- Rule of Law: A system of rules that a society or government develops over time in order to deal with business agreements, social relationships, and crimes.
- Community: All the people who live in a particular area. Also, a particular group of people or part of a society who are alike in some way. Or friendship that is created

VALUES AND BEHAVIORS

      and maintained between people or groups who are different in some way.
- Patriotism: Love of your country, which is often associated with the belief that your nation is better than any other.
- World view: The view that despite national borders all people everywhere have some common interests, traits, and concerns.
- Culture: Ideas, customs, a way of life, and the intellectual and artistic aspects that are produced or shared by a particular society.
- Heritage: All the qualities, traditions, or features of life that have been continued over many years and have passed on from one generation to the next.

B. This category shows some of the behaviors that represent citizenship.
   1. These positive characteristics demonstrate qualities of good citizenship.
      a. The first cluster focuses on the political aspects of citizenship.
- Says the Pledge of Allegiance
- Supports the rule of law
- Votes
- Performs jury duty
- Has political awareness

      b. The second cluster illustrates some social aspects of citizenship.
- Respects other cultures
- Respects other traditions
- Respects other religions
- Has environmental awareness
- Practices recycling
- Volunteers in the community

   2. These measures of conscience and self-control are in support of good citizenship in either a political or social context.
- Doesn't litter
- Doesn't abuse property
- Abides by the law
- Obeys the rules
- Conserves and preserves natural resources

You may feel that the *Three C* lists are incomplete. Your own life experiences have shown you the importance of particular traits that may not appear on the previous lists. As an individual entrepreneur, you are free to add and to emphasize the values that are particularly important to you. As long as we are all dealing with the fundamental matters of *character,*

The Three C's: A Simple System for Grouping Values

civility, and *citizenship* (*The Three C's*), there is room for personal interpretation and individual emphasis.

Likewise, you may look at *The Three C* lists and realize that many of them are known as "virtues." Benjamin Franklin, for example, wrote about the virtues that he believed to be most important; they included sincerity, modesty, calmness, justice, order, and moderation. In fact, he developed a daily program by which he, as an adult, endeavored to practice them so as to make them habitual. He spent time thinking about them and he wrote about his beliefs concerning their importance. Teaching these virtues to children was essential, he felt, to their ability to live a good life.[1]

My concern is also in teaching children, but instead of discussing virtues per se, I choose to emphasize both the expression of positive behaviors and the control of negative behaviors because they work together to demonstrate our values. Isn't that precisely what we want to do—accentuate the positive and eliminate the negative? Remember that it's entirely possible to know what good values are in your mind while you behave in a completely contrary fashion. Children need to learn how to put values into practice.

Why Are Good Values Valuable?

This question goes to the heart of the matter. Why indeed is it worthwhile to learn and to practice good values? Because with standards we know the rules for thinking and behaving. We have more inner strength, more confidence in ourselves. Other people have more confidence in us when they know where we stand. We recognize that we are not alone and that our choices affect other people. We have the capacity to evaluate—circumstances, decisions, choices, and the people around us. We accept responsibility and we acknowledge consequences. We can make plans and set goals because we have enough self-control to follow through.

Let these suggestions prompt your own thoughts. What have your values done for you? Hear yourself sharing these personal results with your grandchildren. Your good values have helped make you the person you are today. Try now to make them simple and specific enough for a child to understand.

VALUES AND BEHAVIORS

What About Situation Ethics?

You and I are aware that morals and values are a topic of considerable discussion and debate in our society.

Because of the era in which we were raised, we know that in order to maintain social stability most of the people must behave most of the time according to shared moral standards called social norms. These days we are more likely to hear about "situation ethics." Many young people have embraced a very flexible interpretation of what is right or wrong depending on the circumstances of a given situation or their feelings about it. They apply this method on a case-by-case basis so that each situation is subject to independent evaluation. They appear to have let go of (or never learned) absolutes for governing the way they behave.

Not long ago I picked up a few groceries and went through an automatic, self-service check out. After scanning and packing my purchases, I put a $20 dollar bill in the pay slot for $13.88 worth of groceries. I received $11.56 in change. When I took my receipt and the money to a human attendant to make things right, she was visibly surprised, informing me that my behavior wasn't at all common. The clerk mentioned that recently a male customer had waved a $5 dollar bill in the air as he announced the "Christmas" gift that he had just awarded himself—extra change that he happily pocketed. This was not unusual according to the clerk. Now, you and I know that's not a "situation"—that's stealing. I wonder if that man's children were with him. I wonder if other children in the vicinity heard. I wonder if anyone talked about the incident.

You may also recognize another common feature of modern life. Our feelings now take precedence over morals. The rules change with the situation and the feelings of the actor. "I feel" has replaced "I know" and "I believe." You can almost hear a popular refrain from the 70s—"If it feels good, do it." The opposite sentiment is also embraced, though without a slogan, which might be—"If you don't like it, forget it." Unfortunately, marriage partners often fall into that category because it also seems to be necessary for significant others to make us happy all the time. Basing decisions, both large and small, on fleeting feelings is about as far as one can go away from the use of moral standards.

What Is Emotional Intelligence?

Emotional Intelligence, a book which received considerable attention when it was published in the mid-90s, dealt with what author Daniel Goleman called a kind of intelligence that is more important than I.Q.[2] The book was described as groundbreaking because it redefined what it means to be smart. The author focused on things other than the traditional I.Q. test, expressing concern for the development of abilities that included self-motivation, controlling one's moods and feelings, a sense of optimism, and the expression of empathy. In his concluding remarks, Goleman conceded that from an old-fashioned point of view, these skills could be summarized in one word: character. He also admitted that self-control and delaying gratification were basic skills that in times past were known as *will power*.[3] Perhaps we are about to come full circle albeit by another name. Character, civility, and self-control may acquire a modern name: emotional intelligence.

You may have occasion to mention the importance of emotional intelligence to the parents of your grandchildren. It can be promoted as a modern concept so that they will be more inclined to find it appealing. Then you can continue teaching old-fashioned values and morals in your new-fashioned way and describe them as features of emotional intelligence.

Now some folks would say that an emphasis on old values is synonymous with a desire to turn back the hands of time. Do you imagine that having traditional values will make the next generation old-fashioned? That doesn't seem at all likely to happen. The future is formed by continuous inspiration, experimentation, and hard work. Life evolves and we are always moving into new situations and new opportunities. Our grandchildren will encounter plenty of surprises along the way. We aren't going to hamper them by supporting and teaching them timeless values. We are going to make their complex lives easier and more certain.

Remember, too, that we all have a strong tendency to idealize the past, and recognition of that tendency should make us question the urge to reproduce the context of old times. As children, we had little comprehension of the full social and political circumstances that affected adult experiences and that makes it easier, in retrospect, to lift memories from their true and complete context. We are not going backward but forward,

VALUES AND BEHAVIORS

along with these young people, enlightened by all of our own experiences of life.

Traditional morals and values are still important because they arm each individual with a solid core of strength and security so that, as a people, the future can be shaped by our best ideals instead of by our worst, most destructive instincts and desires.

In the past, more than now, religious training and participation supported our values in both direct and indirect ways. Children heard old stories and they watched and practiced examples of good behavior. They also absorbed an understanding that the rules apply to a whole community of people who support and perpetuate them.

Belief in a higher power is helpful and comforting. We feel that there is a purpose for the universe and a reason for living. We are given rules for proper conduct which have been handed down through many generations. We feel a sense of continuity with our past instead of feeling isolated and dependent on making up the rules as we go along.

Once again, I want to emphasize your independence as a franchisee. My role is to refrain from dictating a particular religion as the correct choice for *The Business of Life*. That is within your realm and your belief system. Any religious affiliation that you may have should be part of your grandparenting process.

What About Spirituality?

Even though periodic polls show that a large percentage of Americans believe in God, our secular society has tended to embrace the more general concept of spirituality. This means that individual Americans create a personal, more individual way of filling the need for meaning and connection. Whatever you believe, you will probably have occasion to talk with your grandchildren about a higher power. The subject will be part of their lives and they will need to understand. More important, they will need something beyond themselves to believe in. Even kids who go to church regularly will certainly have questions about what it all means and what life is ultimately about.

A CONSULTATION WITH DYLAN

Setting: The back porch of his parents' home in late winter.
Participants: Dylan, age seven, and Grandmother.

The Three C's: A Simple System for Grouping Values

The occasion: Another long-distance trip that was planned to include *The Birthday Program*. (The following dialogue represents only a portion of this event.)

Action: Listen for the slight squeak of the porch swing as Grandmother and Dylan relax after dinner.

Dylan: "I want another cookie, Gramma."

Grandmother (with a look of mock amazement): "Goodness, you can't be serious! Let's just swing for a bit." (She pauses.) "You know, I was surprised and pleased when you said grace before dinner all by yourself."

Dylan (dropping his head and looking sheepish): "I don't always do it, Gramma."

Grandmother (taking and patting his hand): "I know, Sweetheart. But why do we say a prayer before we eat? What does it mean?"

Dylan (looking up into her face with his mouth agape): "Because it says to say thanks for the FOOD!"

Grandmother (attempting to look contrite): "That's exactly right. Now, tell me about God."

Dylan: "He made the whole world."

Grandmother: "Yes, and so we thank him for our food. What else do you know? How does he want us to act?"

Dylan: "Be good and take care of people." (Then a few moments of silence.) "And don't use bad words!"

Grandmother: "Well, those sound like good rules to me."

The conversation continued as Grandmother moved to another topic.

Appreciate the challenge of deciding when to leave a topic and when to expand upon it. Do be gracious and remember that Grandmother was still learning and practicing. She evaluated this session later and felt that it was a bit sparse in content. However, she was pleased that she had made immediate use of a topic that occurred in the natural course of events and that was immediately relevant. In addition, since no topic ever disappears, Grandmother knew that she had learned first-hand more about her grandson's understanding of God and, having made a beginning, she wouldn't hesitate to talk about this subject again in the future.

VALUES AND BEHAVIORS

In one of his last books, Dr Benjamin Spock wrote about rebuilding American values. He believed that, in order to keep spiritual values alive in our culture, it was vital for at least one parent to look towards the future with a sense of optimism. He feared that if this outlook wasn't represented, children would learn to focus on routine, daily matters and that as teenagers they would be inclined to view the world with skepticism and cynicism.[4]

Wouldn't it be wonderful to see your grandchildren become young adults who are generally hopeful and optimistic? These traits are supported by a belief in your own capacity to accomplish your goals, despite occasional fears and doubts. If you are optimistic, you see failure as something that you can remedy. Teenagers, especially, need assurances that they can manage their lives with confidence by taking things step by step and by learning to delay immediate, short-term impulses for longer-term goals.

I believe that we grandparents can and should be good ambassadors for the future. Think about how morose we can become over all of the things that are wrong with our world and how sad and sorry things seem to be at times. Our grandchildren have no comparisons to make; they only have possibilities. Envision the best for them and work to help support the values that will enable them to live a good life.

How Can We Make "The Three C" Concepts Practical?

Think about someone you know whom you would describe as a good person. Think about the specific traits that this person exemplifies. Does this person demonstrate a cluster of traits from *The Three C* list of values and behaviors? Would you say that this person's life meets your definition of a life well-lived? I hope that you are a happy example of your own ideal. Have you made mistakes? I expect so and I trust that you have learned important lessons from them. A good life is always under development. Never forget that our grandchildren will follow this same pattern.

It isn't too difficult to find basic elements among *The Three C's* that describe a committed marriage partner by combining values of *character* and *civility* along with the measures of self-control that prepare one to

The Three C's: A Simple System for Grouping Values

take on that critical role. Of course these characteristics don't guarantee happiness or success, but they do provide a good platform for both.

A different selection of traits might help describe the individual who chooses a public service career or the people who become teachers. They express themselves through the more community-oriented of *The Three C* values. We should find good parents and true friends among those who live by the character- and civility-oriented values. We recognize values by the way people behave at home, at work, and at play.

As you contemplate the potential of your business, think about what you want your grandchild to become, not by specific profession, but as a person who has the character and habits that will make the best use of his or her individual skills and talents in whatever way he or she may choose to express them.

Research confirms what grownups have learned about human nature. People who can deal with life's challenges are confident because they believe in their own capabilities. They are convinced that their lives have meaning and they also believe that they have a great deal of control over their own lives. Typically, they are guided by self-discipline, personal responsibility, and good judgment.[5] Grandmothers and granddads can pitch in by highlighting methods and endorsing processes rather than awards and honors.

In *The Business of Life* we must be prepared to interpret values and morals through behaviors. Remember that all of the important values are revealed in small, daily events. I do not encourage lecturing grandchildren about esoteric adult concepts. Lecturing is useless and is all too often demeaning as well. We will make these concepts practical by talking about everyday experiences in the child's life.

Doesn't Everyone Already Know About Good Values?

As mature adults, we may be too complacent in our assumption that children are simply going to correctly and automatically absorb the preferred adult knowledge about good values and behavior skills. This assumption is natural because it does tend to describe the environment in which we grew up and, therefore, it reflects our experience. This expectation must be relegated to the past. The present lacks a shared, uniform

VALUES AND BEHAVIORS

set of standards practiced by all adults in all aspects of life. Indeed, children do develop in large measure by copying what they see, but today they are going to find a maze of choices and a wide variety of behaviors to consider in all aspects of their lives. At the same time, there are fewer boundaries that limit behavior and fewer signals that clarify preferred behaviors. It is precisely because they do not have a common standard to replicate that we must focus our attention on teaching and reinforcing appropriate behaviors and naming the underlying values as each child grows.

This means that even though you may be generally satisfied with the way their parents are raising them, good values need support from other important people in the child's family. These standards must be larger than mom and dad. They should be demonstrated as effective over generations. They link us to our families and our communities. They serve our country. Ultimately it is the personal responsibility of each of us to live by these values for the good of all of us.

CHAPTER 10. Self-Control

One's first inclination when contemplating values is to consider the kinds of public behavior traits that would be welcomed in a grandchild's behavior—for example, saying please or thank you. However, it is important to recognize that the absence of certain behaviors is often translated into a positive value, as shown in *The Three C* value charts. For example, taking turns means that a person must deny herself or himself the "me first" prerogative in what we recognize as an expression of civility. Another example is found in the person who doesn't litter but, by controlling the impulse to get rid of the refuse in the easiest way possible, demonstrates a sense of community. If we were to turn these into positive values we would find various examples of self-control, self-restraint, or self-denial. This is another more subtle cluster of behaviors that supports the positive expression of many values.

Self-Control

We don't need to ask why self-control is necessary. It is difficult for me to believe that individuals feel good about themselves by proclamation. A torrent of compliments doesn't create a good or happy person nor provide a true self-image. Rather the opposite happens. Every individual achieves a sense of self-respect by holding a set of standards and expectations and then trying to live up to them. Our capacity to mature and to achieve is dependent, in large measure, on our ability to control our impulses. We gain self-worth by challenging ourselves to meet high standards despite problems and failures. We learn to try again and again without giving up easily or cheating. We learn to take responsibility for our failures as well as our successes. Undifferentiated praise does not generate self-respect or self-confidence. Mature adults know this from experience. The process of practicing through trial and error plus accepting consequences that seems so obvious to us has been lost in the eager search for self-gratification. Some child development specialists now feel called upon to reemphasize the old truths we grandparents take for granted.

Isn't some degree of self-evaluation necessary to achieve self-control? Self-satisfaction isn't wrong, but there must be an appropriate place for feelings of shame and remorse in a system which teaches values and personal restraint. Nowadays negative feelings are labeled politically incorrect, as though by refraining from mentioning such sensations we can make ourselves feel good.

During the sixteenth and seventeenth centuries, the Puritans believed in and made a virtue of partaking of all things in moderation so that they gained self-esteem from self-denial. Benjamin Franklin proclaimed moderation a virtue during the eighteenth century. Now, at a time when our culture values the maximization of pleasure, it's a lot more difficult to be proud of yourself for exercising self-control.[1]

Many of us have simply let go of old behavior standards especially when no one is around to observe and disparage us for abandoning them. There is a growing tendency to deny personal responsibility for most anything. What has happened to culpability and the sense of shame? Once upon a time, they were part of our education along with values and morals. Because adults were in charge of this process, children felt the power and authority that adults possessed. Adults knew which words and

VALUES AND BEHAVIORS

deeds were shameful.[2] Children were trained to mimic adults' good behavior.

Today, little is hidden from children. The extent of their new awareness of things once hidden and reserved for adults is primarily the result of new information technology (television, movies and the Internet), affluence, and consumer marketing, plus changes in social attitudes and legal decisions based on adult desires. All these factors contribute to the loss of childhood innocence because it is now very difficult for concerned adults to conceal information and to dole it out as appropriate according to the child's level of development.

Neil Postman, writing in *The Disappearance of Childhood*, associates this gradual decline in shame with the decline of manners in American society. Now we are less inclined to restrain ourselves and to curb what we say in consideration of others. In the past, our sense of shame gave us a reason to control ourselves. Good manners meant that we were deserving of praise and we frequently received it.[3]

The absence of shame in much of modern life may seem to be beyond our individual control. On the other hand, we should respond to our grandchildren in ways that will reinforce their sense of personal responsibility for their words and deeds and their ability to measure their behavior against a firm standard. We can choose whether or not to abandon the politically incorrect term, shame, without giving up our belief in the need for a personal habit of self-correction.

As an illustration, I'm going to describe a situation reported not long ago by the media. It went something like this: a young mother was about to bring a lawsuit against an elementary school teacher and other school officials. The reason given was that her daughter had been embarrassed in front of the class when the woman teacher remarked that the child's fingernails were dirty. The girl reported this incident to her mother who rose forcefully and publicly to her daughter's defense.

Not long ago, you and I would have expected the mother's response to be entirely different and along these lines: in a light, scolding tone mother would say, "Shame on you. You know better than that. Why, germs are growing in that dirt. Now go wash and use the fingernail brush. Then bring me the nail file and the pink polish. We'll make your hands look clean and pretty."

Self-Control

Notice that in the old-style response to this situation, the mother supported the teacher's opinion and confirmed the expected behavior. That is, the social standard at school was the same standard found in the home. Both adults, teacher and mother, knew that the responsibility for compliance belonged to the youngster. The embarrassment suffered by the child was a product of the girl's failure, for whatever reason, to have clean hands and fingernails. Likewise, the responsibility for correcting the situation belonged with the youngster. Shame resulted from knowing the correct behavior and failing to exercise it. This mother would have regarded her daughter's feelings as a clear signal that she felt an appropriate twinge of guilt. She would not want to change that—a far different response from the modern mother.

We have no way of knowing whether or not the modern mother's reaction is quite common or very rare, but it deserves our contemplation. While the incident is small and seemingly insignificant, the modern sample can be transferred and applied to other circumstances with more serious results.

I suggest that grandparents help their grandchildren discover good feelings about themselves that result from the habit of controlling their own behavior within the family and school context. Without using heavy doses of shame, we can endorse the satisfaction of positive feelings about doing the right thing and compare that to the negative feelings within ourselves and the negative reactions of other people that result from our poor choices or actions.

William Bennett, in his recent book on virtues, touched on the rather casual approach in vogue now when we talk about values and how it is important that we have them. We act as though they were "beads on a string" or "marbles in a pouch," he wrote, as though we could all go out and get some.[4] We know, as he does, that values aren't possessions; they are meaningful only when they are a part of who we are, the way we feel about ourselves, and the way we act and live. I was pleased to note that in his listing of ten essential virtues, Bennett chose to begin with self-discipline. I assume that indicates its primary importance in his mind.

How Can We Influence These Behaviors?

Excellence in grandparenting is a matter of being savvy and thoughtful. Think about your spontaneous responses to various situations that

VALUES AND BEHAVIORS

fall between self-indulgence and self-denial. How do you act behind the wheel of a car? Are you patient or aggressive? Do you relax or push the limits?

What about other situations? What are the expectations that you hold about the behavior of your grandchildren when they visit in your home? Do they coincide with the reality you experience when they arrive? Are your standards lenient or strict and do you and your spouse agree on what they are? When should we expect to see signs of social self-control in young children? What kind of expectations did you typically encounter from parents and teachers and how might they relate to today's children?

AN OBSERVATION

The following drama did not directly involve either Grandmother or Grandfather. However, as an observer, Grandmother knew as it happened that she was witnessing an important interaction.

Setting: A summer evening on the deck belonging to another set of grandparents in Dylan's family constellation. These two are avid golfers who teach the sport to youngsters during the summer months. The group, then, includes two sets of grandparents, Dylan's family, and an uncle and cousin who are also present. A meal has just been completed.

Participants: Five-year-old Tyler, who is Dylan's younger brother, and the boys' father.

Action: Grampa comes around the corner of his garage bearing two child-sized golf bags filled with the requisite clubs. He is followed by two ecstatic, whooping cousins, both aged eight.

Background: No doubt these two had "discovered" the new golf sets. Now, everyone present has known for some time that these two youngsters were scheduled for their first, formal lessons come summer and that the younger boy did not qualify for the class. However, when this moment actually arrived, it created a strong response.

Grandmother observes Tyler's initial delight turn to disbelief and then to fury as he realizes that he is not going to be included in this experience. He has not been given a substitute gift and he is forced to face a reality of life.

Self-Control

The action continues: The big boys are the center of attention, but Tyler, a bundle of anger and energy, runs out into the yard. His father calls him back and pats the space next to himself on the bench. The two of them sit side by side. Tyler is scowling and fidgeting while his dad begins to talk quietly.

Without being an obvious eavesdropper, which would require moving closer, Grandmother can only pick up tidbits of the dialogue. She hears Dad express empathy assuring his son that he, too, has felt the same way. She hears that Tyler will have a chance to play golf when he is older, and that he can't always have the same things that his older brother has. There are words about calming down and refraining from doing damage to the golf gear that now belongs to his brother and cousin. Dad says that he knows it's hard to wait until he's big enough to have his turn, but he expresses confidence in Tyler's ability to do so. Tyler leaves the deck to wander around in the big backyard. Before long his brow begins to clear and he returns to the family group. He is somewhat subdued but Grandmother notes that he is adapting well and behaving much more like the open and friendly fellow that he is.

Grandmother moved over and took Tyler's place on the bench. Do you know what she said to the boys' father?

1. How does a grandparent's heart react to a situation like this? Do you feel inclined to provide some gift as soon as possible to assuage Tyler's feelings and let him know that somebody loves him? Squelch the impulse and get ahold of yourself! We, too, must exercise self-control on behalf of an important lesson such as this one. Don't try to counteract this kind of reality because you would be doing any child in a similar situation a great disservice. Every life includes some hard lessons.

2. Do take the opportunity whenever you can to compliment your grandchildren's parents as you observe them teaching good values and life skills.

3. Remember that these events can be recycled. Grandmother now has an excellent opportunity to incorporate this experience into Tyler's next birthday consultation. This youngster demonstrated admirable self-control. His dad gave him an immediate outlet for expressing himself verbally in their private conversation as well as some advice on how to think about what happened plus some hope for his future. Altogether, it

VALUES AND BEHAVIORS

seemed to do the trick. Still, this may well be an experience that Tyler remembers for years to come.

...And When They're Teenagers?

We have already reviewed some of the social changes that affect the lives of teens, but we must begin to translate the generalities into specific material for consulting with them. In doing this we can't help but make comparisons with our own youthful experiences. Ask yourself these questions. What are your honest feelings about the behavior standards for teenagers when you were young? How are those standards affected by the easy availability today of every kind of adult knowledge and temptation? Do more choices and possibilities improve their lives in some ways or? Do more temptations make life harder to master?

We have recently witnessed in the media a reminder that Boomer parents, who experienced their teen years at that time when "sex, drugs, and rock 'n' roll" were the standards, are now parenting teenagers of their own. They face several dilemmas: what to reveal, if anything, about their own behavior as teens and subsequently, for some, whether to lie or tell the truth, as well as the question of what standards to set for the behavior of their own offspring. Their own youthful inclination to indulge hedonistic impulses now puts them in an awkward position. Although they have the opportunity to speak honestly with their children about the damage caused by drugs and casual sex, there are recurring indications that too many of them shy away from talking about these subjects.

Poet and author, Robert Bly seems to believe that there is a dearth of parenting in our society. In *The Sibling Society,* he wrote, "People of all ages are making decisions to avoid the difficulties of maturity."[5] In this view, adults are behaving more like adolescents while adolescents disdain the idea of growing up. We might, therefore, inquire, "Who's in charge here?" Deborah Tannen, linguist and author of *The Argument Culture,* has an answer. She put it this way: "Citizens [of the United States] are like squabbling siblings with no authority figures who can command enough respect to contain and channel their aggressive impulses. It is as if every day is a day with a substitute teacher who cannot control the class and maintain order."[6] In other words, no one is in charge.

As modern grandparents, we would do well to fully realize that teenagers now have access to all kinds of information, and yet we must remember that they do not necessarily have maturity nor ready guidance from busy parents. On the one hand, because of what they appear to know, they cannot be called innocent. Yet, on the other hand, because of their rather limited range of life experiences, they do retain a level of naïveté. This description probably would fit most teens of any decade because of their life stage, but we must be cognizant of their particular social milieu and the cultural context that molds their expectations. In this respect, we cannot afford to assume that they are just like our own children were at that age. Fortunately, with the benefits of hindsight, we are now in a better position to evaluate their true needs when it comes to values and behavior standards that will serve a lifetime.

While you contemplate these things, remember that teens are notoriously skilled at shifting the topic of conversation from present application in their own lives to a grand, philosophical discussion. New-fashioned grandparenting will become old-fashioned quickly unless we go well beyond the simple impulse to argue or demand. We have to learn to be comfortable while engaging in the give and take of genuine conversation about real life and real issues. I believe that our role requires consistency—consistency in our expectations that values are to be learned and lived from the beginning of early childhood, and that self-control is part of the package.

CHAPTER 11. Freedom and Responsibility

A friend recently reported that a group of foreign exchange students, who had come to America to live and study for a semester, were shocked and angered to discover that they were not going to be "free" to do as they pleased at any time of day or night! "I thought this was a free country," one of them groused. The host parents, who took

VALUES AND BEHAVIORS

their responsibility seriously, knew the difference between freedom and license.

Freedom, as noted and discussed in Chapter 8, is probably the most fundamental of our American values. Unfortunately, the meaning has been divorced from political constraints and constitutional authority, and reinterpreted to mean "permission." There are very real signs that freedom is being separated from the notion of responsibility or self-restraint, and the context of freedom has been expanded well beyond the narrow bounds of its original purpose. Without these safeguards and in the absence of definitive guidelines or social norms for behavior, we encounter chaos. The desire to do and say what we please whenever we please isn't limited to foreign visitors. The failure to curb those desires results in lots of verbal garbage that stinks up the culture and lots of people who claim their "rights" to indulge their impulses without regard for others.

What do we, the elders, mean and what kind of behavior do we expect when we ask individuals, including kids and teens, to be accountable for their actions and their speech? Consider the original meaning of the phrase "freedom of speech." In the beginning, it meant that citizens of this new country had the right to disagree publicly with the government regarding issues of government and of public policy. That freedom was supported by the right to back up those private opinions with a private vote. (Voter eligibility has, of course, expanded since that time.) None of us elders confuses these matters with the right to say anything at any time in front of anyone. Can we hope that Americans will learn to recognize the value of freedom of speech while exercising personal restraint in particular circumstances?

In the firm opinion of Dr. Laura Schlessinger, "our freedom consists of mastery over oneself, over our whims, temptations, immediate gratification, self-centeredness, and greed. The freedom to choose challenges us all the time."[1]

Although freedom and responsibility are appropriate philosophical topics for discussion with older children, we know that the basic behaviors relating to the exercise of freedom and restraint exist even in nursery school. Young children can relate to questions that draw out information on the personal and family responsibilities that we all have. They should

Freedom and Responsibility

be familiar with school, playground, and citizenship responsibilities. Remember Dylan and Grandmother talking about litter bugs and respecting school property? These are examples of the responsibilities that accompany some of our rights and freedoms.

Responsibility, in simple terms, means admitting to your own actions although nowadays we say we "own" them. By making our own choices and then accepting the consequences, including those that are negative, we learn to be responsible for our own decisions. Responsibility also means doing what's right without being told or reminded. It means taking care of your possessions and respecting those that belong to other people. It is about helping your family, telling the truth, cleaning up your own mess, and facing things that challenge you. On a more grown-up level it means making choices based on your thoughtful understanding of their probable impact.[2]

Young children, of course, can be expected to deny doing things that may get them in trouble. Older kids will argue that they aren't responsible if their intentions were good. The adult response should be firm. Even if you didn't do it on purpose and even though you may feel sorry, you still have to try to make things right.[3] The experts admit though that this behavior takes lots of time and practice for a youngster to absorb and accept.

Part of the difficulty and confusion comes when parents themselves insist that they are not responsible for many, or even most, of their own actions. Sometimes grownups attempt to cite social conditions beyond their control as a causative factor for their own bad behavior. Some blame advertising as the culprit for their own bad choices when they fail to resist temptation. They are endlessly creative in finding fault outside themselves. Everything is blamed except the individual's own lack of responsibility, effort, will, or commitment. This blame game runs rampant. Personal problems must be the result of bad parenting; happiness is completely dependent on what others provide. One's own intentions are always defined as innocent so that even accidents can be blamed on someone else. Adults turn to the legal system for complaints both large and small. In the meantime, the children are watching and listening and learning.

Actually, it is when we recognize that we are accountable for our own decisions and actions that we have greater control over ourselves and the course of our lives. In other words, the assumption of responsibility

VALUES AND BEHAVIORS

results in a sense of empowerment and is the reverse of victimization. Certainly this is a trait that we want our grandchildren to develop. Being responsible for oneself supports feelings of self-worth and competency which are excellent qualities for a person of good character.[4]

A CONVERSATION WITH CAITLIN

This dialogue preceded a regular *Birthday Program* consultation that took place later in this particular weekend.

Setting: On what promises to be a crisp fall weekend, Grandmother and Grandfather welcome another set of family members who have come to visit them. This group consists of Caitlin, age ten, her sister, Natalie, age six, their five-year-old brother, and their now-single mother. They are frequent visitors because they live only three hours away.

Participants: Caitlin who discovers Grandfather in his workshop.

Caitlin (as she bounces in obviously curious and impressed with the activity underway): "Hey, Gramps! Whatcha doin'?"

Grandfather (with a twinkle in his eye): "That's Grandpa to you, Missy. What does it look like?" (There are boards and tools laying on the worktable.)

Caitlin (taking off her glasses and setting them on a nearby stool): "You're building something . . . a sort of shelf, I . . . "(but Grandpa interrupts.)

Grandfather (frowning): "You can't be putting those glasses there."

Caitlin (looking around): "Why not? They're O.K." (She turns back to face the worktable and begins to look at the materials.)

Grandfather: "No, they're not. You'll probably sit on them. Now put them over here." (He points to a shelf on the wall in front of them which she doesn't notice.) "Those glasses are your tools, and it's up to you to take care of them. They have to be ready to do the job for you."

Caitlin (appearing penitent): "Oh, I guess so. Well, where should I put them?"

Grandpa (scowling now, taps his index finger on the shelf): "They'll be safe right there. Now they're your responsibility. You're the one who needs them. Besides, if they get broken, it'll cost your mother more money." (Caitlin groans.) "Remember your grandmother's old saying, 'A place for everything and everything in its place?' Those are good words to live by."

Caitlin: "Yeah, Gramps, I mean Grandpa." (She smiles and throws her arm on his shoulder as they face the work bench side by side.) "I get it ... really. I'll be more careful."

Later, Grandfather shared this dialogue with Grandmother who decided that she would incorporate another review of responsibility, using a different situation, into her coming *Birthday Program* consultation with Caitlin who has already expressed a desire for contact lenses.

Is Guilt a Bad Word?

What if we fail to meet our responsibilities? What about guilt? Social commentators have noted that it is rather difficult for a child today to be upset by a guilty conscience and many adults don't quite understand what that means.[5] Now, if Caitlin were unable to locate her eyeglasses at some point, she would surely be annoyed. However, she would not feel the pangs of guilt without first having developed a sense of culpability. What would she do in the latter case? Why, she would automatically blame someone else (most likely her mother) for their disappearance. She would not feel personally responsible because her conscience, that internal keeper of the rules, would be silent on the subject.

Our conscience becomes the keeper of our ideal standards. It is the mental message board that serves up moral judgments. In their presence, our failure to act accordingly means that we are worthy of blame and we call that discomforting feeling guilt.

Many people today believe that we should avoid guilt at all costs because it makes us feel bad. Here the first step is to deny responsibility so as to avoid any such consequences. And to think that many of us grew up with the recommendation that we should always let our conscience be our guide!

Saying "I'm sorry" used to be an acknowledgment of personal guilt. How frequently do you hear people say it now in the sense of claiming responsibility, when the speaker means, "I did it and I regret it. It was the wrong thing to do."? A verbal apology was once necessary to set the transgressor on a corrective path of self-improvement. It implied that the

VALUES AND BEHAVIORS

speaker knew right from wrong and would henceforth endeavor to make a proper choice among the alternatives.

Sometimes the error was in the omission of an expected behavior which adults interpreted as thoughtlessness. Such a lack of civility frequently required an apology. There were gradations of seriousness but there was always individual responsibility.

Grandparents remember guilty feelings about youthful transgressions. It seems to me that if we are going to help define what is right and what is wrong, then we can't ignore feelings. We need to discuss these situations and help children discover how to resolve them and get the good feelings back. Without an internal signal of discomfort, we lose the incentive to evaluate our own conduct. And without that ability, we cannot be said to have a personal value system nor can we take the necessary steps to correct our own behavior. We are reduced to selfish motivations and a disregard for fulfilling responsibilities which rightfully belong to us.

Our objective in good grandparenting should be to work with the issue of responsibility from the beginning. We should be eager to talk with our grandchildren about behaviors that demonstrate responsibility and to relate the concept to the daily circumstances of their lives as Grandfather did in his conversation with Caitlin. The sooner we are able to discuss and support this value, the better. Along with issues of self-control, personal responsibility should be part of our consulting program from the earliest stage possible.

SUMMARY

In Part Four, the critical topics of values and behaviors were reviewed with every intention of making the concepts simple and practical for grandparenting. Fortunately, we are all familiar with this territory. Our challenge now is to remember that we will need to think about how to make these concepts relevant for children and teenagers who live in a slightly unfamiliar world.

Next, in Part Five, we will take up a few "business" details so that we can move on to give our full attention to matters that will directly affect our consulting activities.

A JOB DESCRIPTION FOR GRANDPARENTS (Part 3)

We know that tried and true values and moral standards will not prevent any child from being comfortably modern according to the standards of his or her own generation. We aren't going to be cranking out kids who will feel weird or displaced. We want them to embrace the future and look forward to their adult lives with the knowledge and skills that will yield confidence and anticipation. One of our responsibilities is to help them practice.

The foundation for a good life has been expressed in shorthand as *The Three C's*. The values represented are rooted in our history and our American story. They unfold in the ways we care for each other at home and in our communities and for those with whom we share this earth. If we expect America to be and to remain a world leader, we must not neglect issues of *character, civility,* and *citizenship*.

This value element is, therefore, expressed in the next portion of our evolving job description.

BUSINESS OF LIFE GRANDPARENT (Part 3)
JOB CONTENT

An appreciation of fundamental American values is necessary. This may require some active review of values application in the areas of character, civility, and citizenship. An ability to recognize the expression of values through the behaviors of youngsters will maximize results.

(To be continued.)

PART FIVE

BUSINESS PLANNING

It is surprising but often true that a lot of organization and effort goes into the making of something that appears to have occurred spontaneously.

We are headed towards a grandparenting event that must epitomize planned, organized, calculated spontaneity! Think of the time, expense, and learning that teachers undergo before they are deemed prepared to interact with children in a classroom situation.

Teachers exemplify the background preparation that I believe is necessary for a new, "professional" kind of grandparenting. Whoa, you may be thinking. All that just for grandparenting? Well . . . not exactly, because we have previous experience. I do suggest, however, that we review and brush up on some handy techniques so that we will feel confident and comfortable in our new role. Of course, the best teachers are those who love and enjoy children, but remember that love alone doesn't equip them to be successful nor will it suffice for us.

The simple reason that we should take a little time to consider and prepare is that our grandchildren deserve our best efforts when it comes to sharing and discussing life. Those "magic moments" will be more plentiful and more meaningful if we know just what we want to do and have a good idea of how to go about it.

Do Entrepreneurs Actually Bother with This?

You have probably heard about the occasional computer genius who scribbles a few ideas on the back of a napkin and trades it for a few million in start-up costs. Something like that happens, so they say, in Silicon Valley. More often than not, however, the rest of the dreamers have to be a bit more descriptive.

The Business of Life doesn't require real estate, buildings, equipment, or staffing, and we can ignore the typical need for financing. There are, however, several planning elements that will help organize and shape our thinking and our expectations. They will help to bring us together in a shared understanding of our role as we move away from the less demanding requirements of doing what comes naturally.

Perhaps you recall hearing this advice as a youngster: anything worth doing is worth doing well. These days we are more likely to hear the message expressed as a quest for excellence. In either form it is my standard of choice for new-fashioned grandparenting.

As consultants we will want to consider leadership styles and management skills. Perfecting our skills won't make any of us less natural or genuine as grandparents. These skills won't inhibit our spontaneity, either. We will simply increase our ability to do this job with a greater sense of comfort and confidence. Our follow-through will be more effective and more likely to have an impact on our clients. We may not be earning consulting fees, but we had better think about the quality of our performance.

CHAPTER 12. The Mission Statement

At this stage in the development of our new-fashioned grandparenting enterprise several requirements have been identified: the entrepreneurial drive needed to forge ahead, a deficiency/opportunity in the teaching of American values, a review of *The Three C's,* as well as the preparation of our individual market analyses.

The Mission Statement

In corporate America, a *mission statement* is now an accepted and fairly common description that encapsulates the business philosophy. It is a declaration of what the business intends to accomplish and represents the prime focus of the entire enterprise.

For *The Business of Life* I have developed this statement to focus the attention of all individual franchise owners. It is a concise description of the business philosophy and the goal which we intend to achieve. It is worthy of review from time to time as owners may tend to become distracted with functional details.

The Mission Statement summarizes the expectations we have for our modern style of grandparenting and it represents the commitment that enthusiastic adults should be willing to make. It also gives us a group identity. When you meet another *Business of Life* grandparent, you will know just what that person is involved with. You can expect that you share a common perspective about your position in life and that each of you has made a similar commitment. And although you are working alone, it's nice to be certain that there are others just like you out there. Meeting or conversing with other grandparents who are operating a franchise in this system will give each of us a sense of belonging to the larger effort.

THE BUSINESS OF LIFE MISSION STATEMENT

Mission: To improve America one grandchild at a time.

Values: We believe that every child's growth and his or her own talents and skills should be grounded in good character traits, good manners, and a concept of community. *character, civility,* **and** *citizenship* **shall be known and described as** *The Three C's.*

Philosophy: Grandparents have the perspective of maturity and experience which provides us with a unique capacity to guide and teach these values by reinforcing good behavior choices.

Therefore: We shall make it our business to devise a method of sharing this knowledge on a regular basis with each of our grandchildren as they grow. In so doing, we will create a contemporary style of grandparenting with its own grandparenting ritual. Although working as independent individuals with our own grandchildren, by

BUSINESS PLANNING

producing these lessons all across America we will achieve a widespread impact on our society.

The Mission Statement reminds us of critical issues. It summarizes what we are about as an organized group of grandparents as well as the direction in which we are headed as individuals.

Our business name is short, dramatic, and to the point. It implies substance and authority. It succinctly states what the essence of grandparenting is all about.

The Business of Life concept is a serious proposal to organize and standardize a special grandparenting activity. We intend to combine our personal experiences with professional management skills and perform very much like consultants who provide expertise and guidance to real companies. The consultation experience is called *The Birthday Program*.

Grandparents will meet with each "client" grandchild on an annual basis in order to create the circumstances for a special kind of grandparent/grandchild conversation. This private consultation will give you and me the opportunity to share and investigate important experiences and events in the child's life which we will use as the basis for lessons in living.

You have already discovered some of the first elements of the complete job description for grandparents which, when complete, will describe the simple components that are necessary to meet the highest standard of performance.

Practice constantly as you strive to perfect the modern techniques that we will review in the next chapters. Our foundation is set in old-fashioned wisdom, but the process will be enhanced through the use of modern concepts and skills.

CHAPTER 13. Consulting and Leadership

Business executives and professionals acquire specialized training and expertise that lend themselves to independent consulting. As

Consulting and Leadership

specialists in some particular aspect of the business world they can work as advisers to other businesses.

Are you familiar with an organization known as S.C.O.R.E.? The acronym stands for the Service Corps of Retired Executives. These people volunteer to share their expertise with those who are just starting out in the business world. This is an excellent analogy for grandparents to adopt. We are members of the senior corps of life specialists and through *The Business of Life* we have a format for sharing our expertise.

Do you feel a touch of concern about the extent of your knowledge? Do you doubt that you have the necessary expertise? Walk into the business/management section of any large bookstore and note the numbers of books that are available for improving business practices and management. You can even read about the management skills of that fictional English teddy bear, Winnie–the–Pooh[1], or the more rigorous command of Captain Picard on the starship Enterprise.[2] More and more books of this kind are produced regularly. Life is a never-ending process of improvement even for those who lead business organizations. If we simply adopt this attitude of continuous learning and improvement, we grandparents will remain well equipped to serve our clients.

Long gone are those days when you could write your résumé by listing the schools you once attended and the places you have worked with a final note indicating that references would be available on request. Your new-millennium résumé must be a marketing piece. It must emphasize your skills and the circumstances in which you have made use of them. The more range and depth you can demonstrate, the better your prospects will be.

Practice Session

Ask yourself these questions: why would my grandchild want to have my services as a consultant? That is, what do I have to offer—knowledge, skills, experience, philosophy, religious beliefs, plans and dreams, wisdom, etc.—and how can I relate them to the things my grandchild is experiencing today? Be specific. Sell yourself!

1. My objectives, the things I would like to accomplish on this job are:

BUSINESS PLANNING

_____
_____
_____
_____
_____
_____
_____
_____
_____
_____

2. A summary of my capabilities that would be particularly useful for this job are:

_____
_____
_____
_____
_____
_____
_____
_____
_____
_____

3. My key accomplishments, based on the experiences that taught me the most, are:

_____
_____
_____
_____
_____
_____
_____
_____
_____
_____

Based upon your excellent résumé, you now have a fresh appreciation of just how much you can do with the knowledge and skills that you have already acquired. You are going to do a terrific job.

What Should I Know About Consulting?

We are about to review the fundamental skills and issues that will affect our consulting performance. This is necessary because we want others to have confidence in our expertise and to accept us as specialists in *The Business of Life,* and because we, ourselves, need to feel comfortable and confident of our capabilities in this role.

When you give advice to someone who is faced with a choice, you are actually performing as a consultant. Ordinary, everyday occurrences that generate a helpful response can be viewed as a form of consulting.[3]

The word "advice" is key here. A consultant is a person in a position to have some influence over another individual but who does not have direct power to make changes. Go back and read that sentence again. Managers, on the other hand, have more control. In a family hierarchy,

BUSINESS PLANNING

then, we might say that the parents of our grandchildren are the managers, whereas our role is that of the consultant.

Consultants need three kinds of general competency:
1. Technical skills or an area of expertise.
2. Interpersonal skills or the ability to put ideas into words, to listen, to give support, and to disagree reasonably in order to maintain the relationship.
3. Professional skills like listening, problem analysis, goal setting, and carrying out a plan designed to achieve those goals.[4]

All of these points, while taken from a business source, are compatible with *Business of Life* grandparenting, especially the interpersonal skills which are so important. Techniques can't substitute for relationships. Our good intentions will be useless unless we can interact successfully with our clients. We don't want unhappy grandchildren who terminate our services!

Ordinarily in a book about relationships, psychologists and similar mental health professionals would be referred to for relationship insights. The guidance of these traditional experts will fall into place in the following chapters that pertain to child growth and development. However, for now we can adopt a fresh outlook and consider some unorthodox ideas that might enhance our grandparenting businesses.

Take a few minutes now to imagine yourself in this picture by doing IMAGINE: Exercise Number Three.

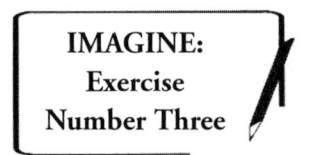

> **IMAGINE:**
> **Exercise**
> **Number Three**

Leadership

Imagine yourself leading a group of people who have been charged by the President of the United States with performing a task of great service to future generations. (You name it according to your interests.)

Consulting and Leadership

You were selected for this job because you have many skills, but you've never done anything of this magnitude before.

WORKSHEET for IMAGINE: Exercise Number Three

Jot down your ideas in response to these questions. How would you begin to handle this assignment? What would you think about? How would you get started? What would you do to get your people to perform and produce?

_____

_____

_____

_____

_____

_____

_____

_____

_____

Relax, superlative grandparenting won't be that difficult, but it will be just as important!

What Is the Modern View of Good Leadership?

In most highly successful companies today, leadership takes place within a business framework that is guided by a clearly identified mission, a set of values accepted company-wide, and a philosophy that recognizes the stakes and equities of employees and involves them in decisions that affect them.

Under these circumstances we find that leaders are people who:
  1. think long-term,
  2. put the customer first,

BUSINESS PLANNING

3. think about the impact of decisions,
4. emphasize the creation of shared values and visions,
5. think win-win,
6. inspire change.[5]

As modern business executives, we *Business of Life* grandparents must be good examples of these simple principles. Let's go through this list from top to bottom and see how they can apply directly to our work.

In the first instance, we are committed to the growth and development of our grandchildren all during childhood and teen years. This kind of grandparenting shouldn't be abandoned on a whim. That corresponds with thinking long-term. Second, we will always put our clients' interests first in our consulting process. This is simply a necessity for any consultant who cares to have a contract renewed. As for the third point, we intend to be prepared and rehearsed so that we may guide the annual event, *The Birthday Program*, toward positive results. Through forethought and planning we will consider the potential impact of each consultation period. The fourth attribute of a good leader is represented by our interest in sharing good values, and we intend to inspire change, the sixth item, by providing direction and by expressing enthusiasm and optimism. Finally, we know that each of us stands to gain as much as we give to the effort which is the essence of a "win-win" strategy, number five on the leadership list.

While all of this is easy to understand, it is not so easy to fulfill. There are numerous training programs available that attempt to discover, guide, and enhance a business manager's inherent leadership qualities. Fortunately, grandparents will draw upon their many years of living, working, dealing with and learning from many types of people.

Give some thought to the way you see yourself as a leader. Does it come naturally to you? It has long been known that personality plays an important part in one's style of leading others. The authoritative style of military leaders, for example, or charismatic leaders, who inspire by sheer force of personality, are easily recognizable. Other leaders naturally tend to invite the participation of subordinates in a more open, consultative style. Through their work, leaders express inherent traits and tendencies which characterize their own individual personalities.

Ideal leaders are seen as people who are driven towards the achievement of strategic goals. They are self-motivated. They have high standards and expectations of their own performance yet appreciate relationships, the needs of others, and working within a group. They tend to be positive and optimistic. Teaching and mentoring are roles they generally fill comfortably.

Each of us has certain personality traits, yet as mature adults we have learned to moderate and adapt as needed to the circumstances of our lives. We have learned many skills and responded to an enormous variety of situations. A grandparent who accepts *The Business of Life* process and its challenges will have many leadership qualities. The entrepreneurial drive itself requires initiative and self-confidence while the process is built upon interactive "people skills."

If any leadership style is to be *avoided* on the basis of its effect on children, a dictatorial approach would be at the top of the list. This style is based on the exercise of power and control. Good grandparenting in our times is not about laying down the law or issuing commands. This style doesn't work long-term in the business world, and it won't work with grandchildren. On the other hand, there is little to be said for the opposite extreme. Failing to have standards or expectations of any kind is not compatible with *The Business of Life* system. Therefore, every consultant must find a leadership style that is both personally comfortable and at the same time is appropriate for dealing with children and teens.

Would Coaching Qualify As a Leadership Style?

In coaching we find a leadership style that Americans know and love. Indeed, sports are often used as a metaphor for life. Participation requires practice, often training by an expert, frequently includes teamwork, standards of excellence, and the satisfactions of improvement and achievement. Organized sports have clear rules that everyone understands. As a coach in *The Business of Life*, you will teach the rules of the game. Even the apparent negative elements of sports activities are part of the necessary learning process as they are in life.

Many youngsters, both male and female, will respond to a sports reference because they feel personally involved either literally, as participants,

BUSINESS PLANNING

or as spectators. It may be easy and comfortable for many adults, as well, to think of *The Business of Life* as a coaching opportunity.

In terms of the coach as a leader, consider the words of a famous National Football League coaching legend, Don Shula, who has described the following as his coaching beliefs:

- Keep winning and losing in perspective.
- Lead by example.
- Go for respect over popularity.
- Value character as well as ability.
- Work hard, but enjoy what you do.[6]

Coaches are experts on the game and its rules and they have a leadership style which guides and inspires others. If the world of sports feels comfortable to you, adopt and adapt this style for your own use in grandparenting. When it comes to your own coaching performance, strive to achieve peak performance or what is called being in "the zone."

When grandchildren actively participate in sports in some way, the grandparent has a very real and potent focus for exploring and endorsing good character values as well as interpersonal values. This holds true whether the child participates in a sport which emphasizes the individual, such as figure skating, or team membership, such as basketball. If the grandparent has also had personal experience in a sport, so much the better. This can be an excellent way to talk about life's lessons in a way that is both direct and relevant for the child or teen.

A TELEPHONE CALL

Setting: Two grandsons are at home in Happy Valley and Grandmother is in another state far, far away.

Background: In the previous week Grandmother and Grandfather had prepared individual surprise packages for Dylan and his brother, Tyler. Each boy received a book about sports that was appropriate for his age and his interests. Earlier in the summer Dylan had taken golf lessons for the first time and Tyler is a basketball fan. A letter, prepared on the computer by Grandfather, had been included for each boy with an appropriate graphic for the each sport. On the day this phone call took place, each youngster took his turn to say thank you.

Consulting and Leadership

Dylan: "Hi, Gramma. Thanks for the book."
Grandmother: "You're welcome. Tell me, can you read it?"
Dylan: "Some of it. Wanna talk with Tyler now?"
Grandmother: "Hold on. I have a question. Do you know who Tiger Woods is?"
Dylan (speaking with great enthusiasm): "He's the greatest golfer in the whole wide world. Well, here's Tyler. 'Bye."

And that was the end of that! By this time, Grandmother has become quite aware that Dylan does not care to talk on the telephone and never has. Tyler, who is younger, seems to enjoy doing so. He speaks carefully and slowly, then listens attentively. Although brothers, they are quite different in this regard.

I wanted to include this terse conversation for several reasons. First, Grandmother would have been irritated and disappointed with the lack of depth in conversing with Dylan except for one factor. She and Dylan have had experience with *The Birthday Program* and she knows that face-to-face, Dylan will carry on an extended, animated, and intelligent conversation. The message is clear. Any grandparent who sees himself or herself in this telephone conversation now has recourse to a better possibility for the enjoyment of a complex conversation with a grandchild like Dylan by using *The Birthday Program.*

Second, Grandmother has no intention of letting this topic go to waste. Not only is it of interest to Dylan and his experiences in learning to play golf, there is also the chance to explore sportsmanship and to talk about what we mean when we call someone a hero. There is every indication that Tiger Woods is just the kind of young man that Dylan would do well to idealize.

Third, Grandmother has time now to develop a cluster of questions for use during her next consultation with Dylan. For the time being, she will make notes and put them in his file. In the next chapter, we will review the style of questions that she will prepare.

The world of promoted and televised sports can also provide many examples of players who make fine heroes by displaying standards that should be emulated. Often, they too are young people with whom grandchildren can identify. Likewise, there are those whose behavior can be a

BUSINESS PLANNING

negative influence. Both positive and negative habits of athletes who are in the news make for lively and substantive discussion topics.

Think about leadership in sports as a discussion topic. Joe Montana, the legendary quarterback, believes that leadership means you must be "willing to take the blame" even though you may not always deserve it. This may be a novel and weird concept for some kids at a time when it is common to avoid accepting responsibility for anything that goes wrong, but it gives a coaching grandparent a good opportunity to discuss an important value. Montana realized that his teammates felt relieved because he refrained from constantly pointing out their errors, in other words, blaming them. He considered his attitude to be part of the meaning of "being a team player."[7]

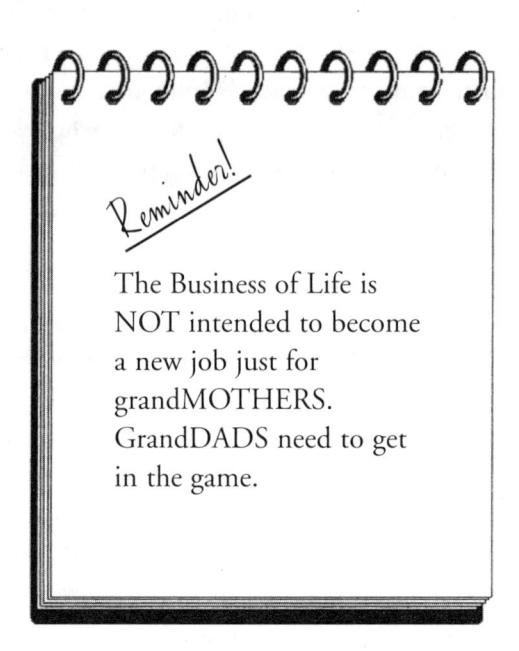

Reminder!

The Business of Life is NOT intended to become a new job just for grandMOTHERS. GrandDADS need to get in the game.

How About Mentoring As a Leadership Style?

Mentoring is currently a fashionable word. It is used in the business arena when referring to someone who teaches skills in a one-on-one situation to a promising employee who would likely benefit from additional guidance and direction. That places it well within the realm of *Business of Life* grandparenting. It is also a process that demands a plan because it is intended to be a productive situation.

Three primary components are needed for successful mentoring in the workplace. They are: mutual trust, patient leadership, and emotional maturity.[8] Much is required of the person who seeks to be an effective mentor. The standards are high. These characteristics are necessary on the part of the mentor because the mentoring process, like grandparenting, is *slow* and at the same time demanding. It takes time. Optimism and enthusiasm are definitely helpful.

A mentor helps the protégé review events and explore the underlying concepts that led to a particular outcome. Mentors help explain situations in light of values and goals.

In a business setting, mentors are expected to understand the ways in which adults learn so that the training can be tailored to fit the recipient. *Business of Life* grandparents have a similar assignment in understanding children for the same purpose.

Dedicated mentors should recognize that no matter what is taught, the protégé is never going to be a perfect reflection of the teacher. The mentor's values and priorities won't be copied exactly. Clones are not produced by the mentoring process. This is a good point to remember whether we grandparents are mentoring, coaching, or consulting. Guiding is quite different from commanding.

CHAPTER 14. Management Skills

Management skills represent the specific techniques that are intended to help us achieve the goals of our leadership philosophy. These skills are fundamentally no different from the management

BUSINESS PLANNING

skills needed to organize a closet, a family vacation, a business trip, a Sunday school lesson, a soccer game, or the purchase of a new home.

Traditional management books once defined four required skills; thus, any manager would be expected to design, organize, direct, and control the programs, projects, and people that were assigned to him. These requirements made a business sound rather like a military operation with managers in command, and a typical business school graduate would expect to operate in this fashion.

Modern management techniques more often focus directly on the art of managing people, and the group that works with a manager is now referred to as a team. You will not be surprised to find that this brings a "coaching" outlook to the role of management. Teamwork sounds more inclusive and more interactive than the old style. The modern view includes things like consensus, collaboration, and group participation.[1] Clearly, good leaders no longer just tell people what to do.

Our criteria for managing won't be based on an aloof attitude of superiority and command which we might have found in the early days of industrialization. In an information-based era we must be able to deal productively with people, especially our grandchildren, and be skilled in working *with* them. This is more demanding but also infinitely more rewarding for them and for us.

Project Management

Often in a business environment, work assignments become projects that must be conducted within a specific period of time and that involve a team of participants who bring differing kinds of expertise to the task. Guidance is provided by a project manager. You can easily see how this description corresponds just as well to a family as it does to a business setting. Nor will you be surprised to learn that a project, as described in a business setting, involves a sequence of tasks to be undertaken within a certain time frame and that it is intended to produce results. Sometimes the resources at hand are limited which can make the task very challenging.

The project manager, having received an assignment, is expected to supply leadership skills in guiding the process. If we think about a single birthday consultation as a project, then it is easy to relate to the manager's job requirements.

Before meeting with his colleagues, the project manager should have a clear vision of the task and be able to set specific goals. Once the project team is assembled, a schedule is prepared, resources are itemized, and tasks are dispersed among the members. Communication throughout the project is a responsibility of the leader as is monitoring progress. At the completion of the assignment, the manager should acknowledge achievements and the successes that the group has produced.[2]

Business of Life grandparents will be able to describe themselves as professional project managers. The personality traits that are considered to be preferable for such work include enthusiasm, a tolerant attitude that encourages partnerships, and a customer focus. No less important is the creation of a vision that can be shared with the client in a way that inspires.

Conducting Meetings

Effective and regular meetings between you, as the consultant, and your grandchild, as the client, are the key to the modern grandparenting business. In creating and conducting effective meetings each grandparent must assume the responsibility for soliciting and sharing information.

Some of the basics for conducting effective and productive meetings in a business setting will apply to our work. There are two basic meeting types which are described as: information sharing and problem solving. Your repertoire as a consultant should include both types.

The location for your meeting and the facilities at hand will have some influence on the outcome. Seclusion and physical comfort leave attention free for discussing ideas, and we should keep this point in mind for our purposes remembering that Grandfather sometimes felt the need to make sure that Grandmother and Dylan were not interrupted. Grandmothers, of course, may also extend this courtesy.

Preparation is the key to a successful business meeting and this, too, is perfectly true for *Business of Life* consulting.

A facilitator is someone who manages a business meeting so as to keep the participants focused on the agenda items. If things get side-tracked, the facilitator restates the purpose of the meetings. A good facilitator would restate information in order to clarify the ideas or conclusions. This person would finalize the meeting by summarizing the content and by reviewing assignments.

BUSINESS PLANNING

While this description may seem to be perfectly obvious as a management skill, it is unfortunately true that many meetings are poorly managed, the follow-through is often weak, or the very purpose of the meeting was vague to begin with. It would be a shame to allow any of these deficiencies to ruin *The Birthday Program*. Think of yourself as the leader who employs the guidance techniques of a meeting facilitator.

Because *The Business of Life* uses a special, annual meeting focused on the grandchild's birthday and because the attention span of young children is rather limited, time is very important. In turn, that means thoughtful preparation will be necessary if you truly intend to be successful in hosting a conversation that includes an example of *character* values, of *civil* behaviors, and of *citizenship* activities.

Do grab any opportunity that comes your way, at any time, to practice focused, mini-interactions with your grandchildren. There is no sense in ignoring a perfect opening. Teachers among us know that dealing with youngsters requires as much skill and preparation as does any meeting attended by adults and that excellence requires practice.

Interviewing

Interviewing is another management skill, one that we routinely associate with the hiring of new employees. However, the same techniques are useful in most effective human communication.

If we wish to elicit or share information in a business or personal setting, dialogue flows more easily through the use of open-ended questions. When we begin a question by using "who, what, where, when, why, or how" we are using the open-ended style. These words invite the other person to talk more freely and at some length because a simple "yes" or "no" doesn't make sense. Open-ended questions help to create rapport. The interviewer can expand on the comments to extend the topic. Conversely, a closed-ended question is answered by a simple "yes" or "no." The interviewer has to be ready immediately with a follow-up question. Now, a closed-ended question has its place and is certainly necessary and appropriate at times. However, a true conversation cannot be said to exist if one person is limited to only short responses.

Practice forming both types of questions using topics that a particular grandchild would like. For example, "What does stealing mean?" would be an open-ended question whereas, "Do you like ice-cream?" would be a closed-ended example.

When an interviewer or a grandparent uses a probing question style the intent is to acquire more detail about the current topic. Asking for an example is a probing technique. This helps draw out details and it gives the consultant a specific situation to deal with in formulating more questions.

Whether in a meeting or an interview, the manager may choose to restate information in order to check on her or his understanding of the content. This means that you repeat what the other person said in your own words and then you ask if you understand correctly. Restatement is a nice way to let the other person know that you have been listening. Grandfather, for example, restated the meaning of responsibility in his conversation with Caitlin concerning care of her eyeglasses, and he even introduced an aphorism ("A place for everything and everything in its place.") to reinforce the meaning.

In summary, skillful interviewing techniques include these styles of seeking information.

- Open-ended questions encourage the respondent to talk freely. They begin with "who, what, where, when, why, or how."
- Closed-ended questions elicit short, simple responses like "yes" or "no."
- Probing questions seek specific information. You might say, "Could you give me an example of that?"
- Restatement is a response that repeats the essence of the other person's comments in your own words to clarify understanding.

A skillful grandparent may sometimes structure questions so as to learn specifics about a situation and to determine both how the youngster acted under the circumstances and the outcome of the situation. Let's review a sample topic that is used throughout the following exchange which is known as a "situation-action-result" sequence.

The interviewer could ask an open-ended question, in child-friendly words, about an event at school. You might want to begin with, "What

BUSINESS PLANNING

did you learn?" and "What will you try next time?" and "I want to hear all about it!" (meaning, what was the situation?), follow with a probing question to narrow the response and focus on the action taken (What did you do?) and then return to an open-ended question to discover the outcome (What happened next?). Finally, restate the sequence in simple words to ensure mutual understanding to complete the sequence. This is an action-packed exchange. It is both immediate and productive.

As a grandparent who wants the most from an organized conversation with a grandchild, these interviewing skills will be very helpful in order to guide and control the content. Practice ahead of time so that you will be prepared with several open-ended questions to get the conversation going. Listen for opportunities to probe further when something is mentioned that seems to hint at a hidden topic that is important to your grandchild. It might be a problem or difficulty. Don't hesitate to pursue things that bring joy as well! Make appropriate use of closed-ended questions when you want a commitment from the child to exercise self-control, for example, or to practice a particular behavior, such as saying please and thank you.

Although there may be times when it will be appropriate for you to do the talking, the primary activity for grandparents in our business meetings is a combination of skillful questioning and "active listening." Active listening utilizes the business interviewer's techniques because you make use of the information you receive in response to your careful questions to develop more questions. This keeps the child talking and the interaction flows along. If the topic moves off track, you either bring it back by the next question that you pose or you follow along and develop a new line of inquiry. All the while, you are alert to the expression of good traits and behaviors and you weave them into the conversation as best you can. When a topic has been depleted, you pick up another theme from your prepared list and begin again with an open-ended question.

Take a "time out" and work with IMAGINE: Exercise Number Four.

> **IMAGINE:**
> **Exercise**
> **Number Four**

Interviewing

Imagine yourself in this new and exciting *Business of Life* consulting role. You feel comfortable about your own leadership style. Your market research has given you a wealth of material. You are thinking of ways to incorporate *The Three C's* into your conversation.

Imagine a suitable time and place either in your own home or that of your grandchild. Create a fantasy conversation where you are the guide. You ask open-ended questions, listen, probe for details, and restate what you hear. Clarify your expectations for the coming year and summarize.

Remember that lecturing is not on the agenda. Imagine the two of you having a wonderful time!

WORKSHEET for IMAGINE: Exercise Number Four

First, begin by writing down a single topic and a related value that you imagine would intrigue your grandchild. Next, create at least one open-ended question about this topic and jot it down. Then write down a probing comment.

1. The topic is:

_____

_____.

2. The value is:

_____

_____.

BUSINESS PLANNING

3. An open-ended question would be:

_____

_____

_____.

4. A probing question would be:

_____.

Using additional paper, do the same exercise with more topics until you feel comfortable in your understanding of question types and when to use them.

Second, perform a reality check on your interviewing skills. Use them in the very next conversation that you have with an adult. Focus on asking an open-ended question and then listen. Follow up with another open-ended question on the same subject. Insert a probing query. Try a closed-ended question but follow that with another open-ended question. Try a restatement if you don't understand. (Or pretend that you don't understand just to experiment.) How long can you keep the other person talking?

Critique your own performance. How well did you do? Did it feel comfortable?

Try this assignment with a child or a teenager and keep practicing.

Performance Reports

I want to make a final comment about a standard management responsibility, the preparation of an employee's performance report. On the surface it would seem to have some bearing on *The Business of Life Annual Meeting*.

A performance report, as used in the business world, is intended to review and to evaluate the employee's job performance during the past year. It is intended to be used as a tool for detecting problems and as a record of achievements. Many believe that it also motivates employees to make improvements. The employee must sign the report to verify that it was reviewed with the manager, and the report is sent to a permanent personnel file. It is a very, very common management function.

While conceptually the performance report may seem like a good mechanism for evaluation, it misses the mark for effective grandparenting, and I recommend that this format be avoided.

CHAPTER 15. Business Philosophy

By refusing to limit our thinking to traditional sources of wisdom, we continue to utilize an entrepreneurial perspective. Let's roam off in another direction, take a left turn, and visit the manufacturing floor of a large company. Here we will discover a modern business philosophy that is transforming manufacturing production systems. Who would expect that we could find a direction for the future of grandparenting in such a location? Aren't you curious?

Lean Thinking

This sounds like the philosophy of some diet program. Actually, that isn't far off the mark. In the manufacturing arena, lean thinking represents a profoundly new way of doing business that could be described as streamlining operations. The terms "lean thinking" or "lean manufacturing" have been adapted from the Japanese. It all began in the United States with a book about the automobile industry published in the early 1990s titled, *The Machine That Changed the World*.

What does the phrase "lean thinking" mean and how can it possibly relate to grandparenting? Lean thinking is relevant because it shows business managers and grandparents how to be frugal and to do more with less. It's actually refreshing because the reason for doing this is to get better and better at providing customers with exactly what they want, precisely when they need it.[1]

Businesses are counseled to reduce complex systems to the bare essentials by eliminating wasteful operations. *Business of Life* grandparents will avoid confusion by staying focused. Focusing on the essence of the business, in manufacturing and in grandparenting, means that it is necessary

BUSINESS PLANNING

to identify only those essential elements that are required to produce the product and to clear away the rest.

From our point of view, this is the same kind of waste reduction and reorganization that is going into the *Business of Life* version of modern grandparenting. I assure you that I do not recommend the elimination all of the many things that grandparents love to do for and with their grandchildren. Reading stories, playing ball or chess, and having tea parties are *not* a waste of time. They are important and they can be fun and I enjoy them too, when I can. Yet, I want grandparents to notice what *should* be done without question and without fail. As you know, I challenged myself to look for the one fundamental and primary thing in life that only we, the elders, can do. Just as lean thinking has changed American manufacturing, *The Birthday Program* changes our perception of our role.

There are even more parallels to contemplate. Ultimately, lean thinking, in a manufacturing setting, affects parts suppliers and distributors because manufacturing flows on a "pull" system.[2] What does that mean? It means that managers are trained to recognize value as defined by the customer and to focus every activity on satisfying that demand. Customer orders are said to "pull" the product through the system by defining what they want as the end product. Customer demand affects the suppliers and distributors as well as manufacturers. It becomes second nature for all participants to acknowledge that the customer is the reason for producing. Unless you are familiar with the business of manufacturing products this may seem strange. How, you may ask, is this different from before?

In the past, companies produced as much as they could and stored whatever wasn't sold immediately. If you are a stock market investor or a computer user, you probably know about the success of Dell Computer, a company which builds product only for a specific customer order. You phone Dell, you describe exactly what you want, Dell makes it and sends it to you. That's the pull system. One customer—one order, and a specific, tailor-made product is the result. Computer companies who used the old system were caught with big inventories of "one size fits all" products that became obsolete sitting on retailers' shelves. That's expensive and it sure doesn't fulfill individual customer preferences.

Business Philosophy

Well, how does the concept of "pull" relate to grandparenting? It coincides precisely with our determination to be informed and to respond to the needs of each grandchild rather than to dispense irrelevant and unwanted information. There is no "one size fits all" lecture series dispensed by a guru at your franchise headquarters' office. The "pull" system means that every individual grandparent tailors each birthday discussion to a specific grandchild because the grandparent has made the effort to become intimately acquainted with that child's experiences and environment. Our goal, together and as individuals, is to serve the needs of each client to the best of our abilities. And we are taking steps to hone our abilities for the provision of superior service.

If you are a long distance grandparent, you must adapt to this modern lifestyle. With limited time and opportunity, lean grandparenting helps you get the most out of every chance that you have to spend time with your grandchild. You can choose to let some activities fall by the wayside in favor of a consultation that will enhance your relationship. Conversely, if you have all the time in the world, carve out the small portion needed to participate in *The Business of Life*. Don't be entirely seduced by all those extra activities. Learn to "think lean" and take care of what is vitally important because your client needs you. Get down to basics just like other business managers who have multiple responsibilities.

As busy consultants with busy clients, we have to make our meetings count. By committing to a series of annual meetings as each grandchild grows, grandparents can replicate the Japanese concept of Kaizen instead of KaiKaKu.[3] This means emphasizing the importance of continuous, incremental improvement (Kaizen) as opposed to sudden, radical improvement (KaiKaKu). In *The Business of Life* there will be a natural sequence for continuous, incremental review of the child's experiences through *The Birthday Program*, because we are wise enough to know that growth and change do not occur overnight.

The quasi-formal consultation, during which you serve as a life-skills consultant, is an event that has been designed to take place once every year, year after year. And every year, you will summarize the highlights in the album, *My Book of Birthdays*. This repetition will give you the opportunity to put all of your knowledge and skills as a leader/manager into play in a child-friendly leadership style while conducting a lively review

BUSINESS PLANNING

and analysis of the events and lessons that your grandchild experienced during the previous year. Lay a good foundation for your annual meeting by conversing often during the year.

This grandparenting process gives new meaning and a unique twist to the concept of lean thinking.

Reframing Organizations

While we are looking at precedents in the business world for engaging in our own entrepreneurial mission, we might also consider the recent suggestion that organizations can be "reframed."

Think about it this way: managers are creatures of habit. They get stuck in ruts. They suffer from the inability to use multiple points of view. Managers too often become complacent. They relax and fail to bring new ideas to the challenges they face. They forget about looking at old problems in new ways.[4]

We, too, get stuck in mental ruts, in relationships as well as in our work. This stagnant condition could be used to describe many of us elders. As we get older we all tend to cling to old ways and old habits. Reframing is another way to characterize the entire *Business of Life* effort. We're shaking things up a bit in order to introduce a fresh outlook towards the age-old subject of grandparenting. As practitioners and entrepreneurs, we recognize the necessity for a change in our assumptions about this familiar role, and therefore, we are reframing the old-fashioned leadership style as well as the process of grandparenting.

Without rejecting the traditional activities, we can add a new dimension and a new process to the role because we understand that a different perspective is necessary under current social circumstances. New times call for new responses and new attitudes. In other words, as grandparents who expect to be effective, we have a contemporary responsibility to alter the former role by introducing a new leadership style.

No longer will we simply react to our grandchildren. Rather we will take the initiative and engage them in something new—not just for the sake of being creative or different. The goal is to be effective so that our new-fashioned role is supportive of their real need to learn and to know about life.

SUMMARY

In this part, Part Five, a *mission statement* was used to summarize our purpose. Consulting standards and styles were discussed, and then critical management skills were reviewed.

Client evaluation will be the focus of Part Six. Our grandparenting interests will lie in the mental, moral, social, and physical stages of child development because we will need to understand our grandchildren's learning capacities.

A JOB DESCRIPTION FOR GRANDPARENTS (Part 4)

We have taken a good look at three essential blocks of material that are components of our new, modern grandparenting activity: business leadership, management skills, and business philosophy.

In this *Business of Life* proposal, grandparenting is viewed as a specialized, professional role which offers the opportunity for discussing important issues in a grandchild's life during a private conversation. If all of this seems serious, it is because we intend to establish a new level of respect for the job of grandparent. While others, who have not had the good fortune to be grandparents, might view this as tedious and heavy-handed, we know for certain that those real, live, exuberant children will make the task fun and keep it filled with surprises.

BUSINESS OF LIFE GRANDPARENT (Part 4)

JOB CONTENT

Every practitioner must agree in principle with the mission statement and be ready to put it into practice.

A comfortable familiarity with modern leadership concepts must be demonstrated and applicable management skills must be sharpened for successful implementation of the mission. If necessary, remedial exercises may be required.

(To be continued.)

PART SIX

CLIENT EVALUATION

Most adults recognize the adage, "know thyself." That is an excellent directive for *Business of Life* consultants. It is also imperative that you make every effort to "know thy client." Client evaluation is similar to market analysis. There is a general level of information (the big picture) and then there are individual children to be considered (family snapshots).

This exercise in client evaluation will give us a good, basic understanding of our grandchildren's general capabilities, according to specialists, and it will enable us to recognize the general developmental stages of childhood and teen years. We will be better able to anticipate subsequent stages and be prepared as our grandchildren move through the expected sequence of growth and development. We can't be concerned only with physical development, however, because we will need to appreciate the normal flow of mental and moral development, as well.

Grandparents are known to be enchanted with their own grandchildren, and I am no exception. To us they are unique and special, and they always seem to be far beyond other children of the same age in their development. They amaze us! Grandchildren tend to be willing and satisfied recipients of this adoration. In this vein, it is far too easy to neglect or ignore what may be important underlying issues in their lives.

CLIENT EVALUATION

Viewing these youngsters as clients is a way to help us temporarily separate our natural emotional responses from our thinking and speaking. I don't want anyone to become callous, rather I recommend that the annual birthday discussion is the time to be more rational and thoughtful. It is important to strive for balance here. This balance may be even more important during the early teen years of our clients. By that time, I hope that you will have practiced and perfected a conversational style that emphasizes thoughtful contemplation of issues rather than emotional lecturing.

If we view grandchildren as clients, at least on the occasion of this special event, *The Birthday Program*, we can step into a more profound level of grandparenting. Through the use of this consulting role, we can bring objectivity to the interaction in order to talk about those things that really count in life. Remember our goal is to coach, mentor, and teach. Loving attention is not being discouraged here. Rather, the intent is to promote and include thoughtful, considerate conversation in a loving, supportive atmosphere.

As you may know, in the business arena there is also an emphasis on the personal growth and development of employees. Once again, we will look for direction and ideas from a business perspective.

Just as we began our market research with a view towards the "big picture" in terms of broad social features, our first foray into client assessment will be a general one. Following this material, we will review some of the more common interests and activities of each age group

CHAPTER 16. Human Development

The development of our human potential is a life-long enterprise, and it is not surprising to find that the continuing development of employees is of interest to business owners.

The human resources department in most large companies includes staff who organize training programs for employees' growth and development.

Human Development

Their goal is to improve the company by improving individuals and their performance. Note the parallel between developing employees to improve a company and developing grandchildren to improve society.

A good program in the adult business setting would include these features:

- a variety of learning methods,
- a moderate level of content,
- a balance between skills, knowledge, and ideas,
- and utilization of the participants' expertise along with a focus on real-life problem solving.[1]

The material used in a business situation is intended to be practical and useful on the job. The more successful programs have a good foundation based on adult learning theory.

If we transfer these ideas to grandparenting, human resource development standards suggest that our job qualifications should include a general understanding of the development of the intelligence and learning capabilities of our client group, our grandchildren. This knowledge should then help provide us with realistic expectations regarding the kinds of responses that we should anticipate from them and the complexity of the comments and ideas that we can share with them.

Clearly, we will be dealing with grandchildren across a wide range of ages and developmental stages. At the same time, we would be wise to remember that individual children respond to different teaching/learning methods just as adults show different preferences. Coaching, for example, was mentioned as an option in our review of leadership styles, but it will not prove to be the best style in every case.

If we know that a moderate level of program content is advisable for adults, then we can assume that a simple level is appropriate for young children, although teens and young adults can accept more content.

From your market research, you will realize that there is a great deal of material from which to select your topics. When you review the general development information in each of the next four chapters, you will be reminded of even more things to talk about.

CLIENT EVALUATION

As you jot them down, consider searching your list and selecting one topic based on the acquisition of new skills, another on general knowledge, and another on an experience involving others—a social type of activity. This pattern can help maintain variety, and it gives a grandchild opportunities to remember and review different kinds of learning experiences. Just like trainers in adult learning situations, we must elicit our clients' expertise by discussing their own experiences and ideas. You and I, of course, will strive to correlate values with these topics and to incorporate them in the discussion.

As you critique your own *Birthday Program* performances, you will discover that some topics you had intended to include were completely forgotten or had to be abandoned because your client became restless or wanted to talk about something else entirely. This can be very frustrating, but it can sometimes evolve into a fruitful exchange when something is of immediate concern or interest to the youngster. You may be handed a golden opportunity to get at something truly meaningful. Conversely, you may be subjected to random babble. In the latter case, your firm guidance will get things back on track.

Remind yourself that talking about some of the issues is better than never talking about anything important. It is a challenge to maintain a balance among the child's experiences, skills, knowledge, interests, problems, and ideas. All of them are generally appropriate for *The Business of Life* process.

Grandparents don't require the depth of information that a child development expert would apply to this task, but a review of the basics will help keep our expectations in line with reality.

What Are the Components of Growth and Development?

In order to be effective *Business of Life* consultants, it's necessary that we try to tailor the message to the child. If we intend to find and support fundamental values as they are expressed in the normal behaviors and activities of each age group, we must know what to expect in order to craft an appropriate response. We must be relentlessly practical in this regard. Because we won't actually be parenting, a more general approach will suffice for our needs. It is true that we have "been there and done that" but it's been a while, and our memories may be less than precise.

Human Development

As an independent entrepreneur, you are encouraged to explore contemporary literature on child development. Almost all of it deals with parenting because no one has imagined that grandparents might play a focused role in teaching their grandchildren values and life skills. Still, we can make use of the information while knowing that our own management style may well be different from that of their parents.

In each of four separate chapters, we will review the mental, moral, and general development of a selected age group. I followed my own advice in preparing this material by reviewing two textbooks[2,3] for general information on growth and development as well as particular books from various experts on more specific topics.

The groupings are:

> Childhood during the ages 4 through 7,
> Youth during the ages 8 through 11,
> Early adolescence during the ages 12 through 15,
> Late adolescence during the ages 16 through 19.

Keep in mind that these age boundaries are somewhat general, but they will serve as a good guide for most children.

We begin with basic definitions in general terms.

Mental Development

Cognitive or "thinking" development is the process by which knowledge is acquired and classified. In our culture, this is expected to coincide with stages of physical development. This means that we do not expect a four-year-old to think like a grownup; that is, by a rational process or to understand adult words that represent abstract concepts. Most four-year-olds cannot multiply numbers nor can they define honesty. Instead, we would expect spontaneity and imaginative thinking, for example, because the child has not developed the level of mental capacity for analytical thought. Remember that young children often mix fact and fantasy simply because they are in the process of learning the difference.

The point of this exercise is to appreciate the flow of mental development from simple thinking patterns to ever more complex ways of perceiving and evaluating information. A textbook or dictionary definition of cognitive development tells us that we will be looking at such things

CLIENT EVALUATION

as awareness, perception, reasoning, and judgment. The original, modern theorist and researcher in this area was developmental psychologist Jean Piaget, whose ideas have been widely adopted. His work was based on many, many experiments with children.

Now we are inclined to consider the more recent findings of other researchers. The concept of multiple intelligences, for example, has been proposed by Howard Gardner, who is also a developmental psychologist. In Gardner's opinion, Piaget was focused only on a logical-mathematical type of intelligence whereas there are other types that, taken altogether, give a more complete description of human capabilities. Gardner includes abilities such as linguistic intelligence as exemplified by poets and spatial intelligence that would be a characteristic of engineers or sculptors, for example.[4]

Despite the recent work of Gardner and many others, our educational system is still primarily geared towards the I.Q. test as the definition of intelligence, and Piaget's work will be reflected in the following general descriptions of mental development. Other specialists will provide information to help round out a general picture of mental abilities as they apply to everyday life.

Moral Development

The second focus in growth and development is on moral development. Recognize that a process comparable to mental development occurs in moral development.

In addition to his well-known work on intelligence, Piaget also published a book on moral development in the 1920s. He believed that mental development had an influence on the ability to make moral judgements. Kohlberg's subsequent work in the area of moral development is also well known and is generally found in textbooks along with that of Piaget. Both of these men found evidence of a clear progression of moral comprehension that begins with simple, universal beliefs about right and wrong and eventually progresses to more theoretical matters. Prior to their research, moral development was the province of philosophers and theologians.

The general descriptions of moral development in the following chapters are given with a view towards practicality and the actual experiences of childhood in order to make them most useful for our needs.

Human Development

Will The Birthday Program Benefit from This Information?

This trajectory in the development of thinking skills and moral concepts, from simple to more complex, seems obvious. However, it is sometimes easy to forget that it is a normal progression when we see the amazing speed at which children grow physically. Because of their sheer size, we grandparents may mistakenly assume that their mental abilities and their knowledge of values and morals are far greater than they really are. And, of course, because they are "ours" we want to believe that this is true. Be on guard against this kind of self-congratulation; it can ruin the very service you are there to provide.

Remember that we have a very practical reason for acknowledging the normal flow of development. Even though many very young kids can mimic adult words, there is no sense in expecting children to think with a sophistication and maturity of which they are not yet capable. *The Birthday Program* must be tailored to *their* capacities. This is a cornerstone of successful communication with children, and it is clearly our responsibility to recognize it and to utilize it.

The neighborhood grocery store, garden center, or hardware store has, by now, provided each of us with at least one example (and probably many) of the unfortunate failure on the part of a parent to appreciate the stages of cognitive development. No doubt you have heard a young parent begin to berate a toddler for some misbehavior. The wailing escalates as the parent speaks more forcefully in adult language and concepts, and the child begins to scream. You and I know that the child is probably bewildered and frightened, and the parent is probably tired, frustrated, and embarrassed. It appears, however, that this parent has poor parenting skills and probably holds little comprehension of the fact that small children are not miniature adults. In most of these cases, the parent appears to be sadly deficient in understanding the nature of the child's thinking abilities, language skills, and moral development.

Grandparents must remember and adjust to the actual level of each child's development. This also means that we must be careful when we equate exceptional verbal skills in a young child with advanced maturity. Train yourself to keep the general standards of development in mind to serve as your guide.

CLIENT EVALUATION

Where Do Personality Differences Fit In?

Good question. Even as we contemplate the normal sequences of mental and moral development which all children must experience, we also anticipate and enjoy the amazing and unique individuality of our grandchildren and their special abilities, talents, and temperaments.

Just as human resource specialists and business managers learn to identify the primary ways in which most adults tend to think and behave, grandparents will recognize the individual behavior styles that youngsters begin to exhibit early in their lives. Whatever the books may say about general growth and development, it is still important to remember that individuals have different personalities.

Once we are grown up we are said to be one of these types:

- Authority-driven people tend to prefer specific direction from an authority figure.
- Deductive thinkers prefer to analyze and are open to logic.
- Sensory thinkers are often "hands-on" people.
- Emotional types relate primarily to their feelings about an experience or assignment.
- Intuitive people have an unconscious process that seems to give them a sense of how to proceed that "just feels right."
- Scientific types want to experiment and to test things for themselves.[5]

Do you find yourself in one of these categories? Perhaps you will begin to recognize and appreciate more of these fundamental differences among people as *The Birthday Program* gets underway and your understanding of each grandchild increases.

What Does All This Mean to a Business of Life Consultant?

In the next four chapters you will be able to review some of the characteristic issues, activities, and concerns which are associated with each age group. The purpose is not only to refresh our minds about what children do and how they think. The key point here is that we are going to overlay another issue on this knowledge.

Development in Childhood

You and I need to be prepared so that each of us can introduce and incorporate *The Three C's* into our annual conversations in a natural and seamless manner. Remembering that values are represented in word, deed, and attitude, we must be prepared to make these value/behavior connections as we talk about the real world in which each individual child is involved.

We must talk about values with care and skill:

- by relating them to the activities the youngsters are engaged in,
- by relating them to the feelings that they have,
- by simultaneously using our knowledge of their capacity to understand, and
- by using language that they comprehend.

I recommend that, for now, you read straight through every chapter, covering ages four through nineteen, even though some of it may not be immediately useful. Later you can return and concentrate on the age range that will be relevant to your next consultation.

CHAPTER 17. Development in Childhood, Ages 4 Through 7

Based on my own experience, the attempt to begin a consulting process is best left until your grandchild is about four years old. Of course, you can experiment and practice at an earlier age and you may be successful. Certainly there are plenty of lessons in nursery school and preschool to talk about. The question of just when to begin is an individual decision based on your own, very individual, client.

Mental Development

These children are still learning the names of many things. They are growing in the ability to represent concrete objects in symbols and words. However, if you were to ask a four-year-old what she did at

CLIENT EVALUATION

playschool that day, she wouldn't be able to give much of an answer. This is simply because of her level of cognitive development. She doesn't have the ability to organize her memories of events in a coherent manner. But if you were to ask her specific questions, she could probably answer them one at a time. This is called the intuitive stage, when problems are not yet solved by logic.

These children are learning how to read by transforming those lines and circles into words.

Roughly between five and seven years, due to brain development, children acquire new thinking capacity. They are able to let go of the information that they receive from their senses like looking and touching and to substitute a new level of rational thinking. For example, if you were to pour a cup of water into a tall, thin glass in front of your grandchild, and another cup of water into a short, fat glass, you could determine whether she had made this transition. Simply ask which glass contains more water. Before this transition takes place, children believe that the tall glass has more water because their eyes tell them so. The water is higher off the table in the tall glass. After this growth period, children can figure out that the same amount of water was poured in both cases and that the shape of the containers only makes them appear to be different.[1]

Here is an example of this new level of thinking that is guaranteed to tug at a grandparent's heartstrings. Literal thinking is needed to believe in Santa Claus. It isn't simply a matter of innocence. By around seven years of age, mental growth advances to include the use of simple forms of logic. Children apply this logic to Santa's delivery of Christmas presents. They begin to notice practical difficulties such as the size of the chimney, the number of presents that the sleigh must hold compared with the number of children all over the world, and the limited amount of time available in one night for a trip around the globe. They come to reject the magic and see reality. This discovery often makes children feel very grown up and eager to inform younger siblings of their discovery.[2]

During this period, children are learning about the titles and relationships of various extended family members, and they may encounter the matter of death, perhaps as a great-grandparent passes on. Before the mental shift occurs, kids can't comprehend the meaning of death or its finality. Their perception of time is entirely different from that of adults. They may accept an adult explanation at one point but later ask when the person is coming back or waking up. After the mental growth transition, they will have a preliminary grasp of the meaning of death.[3]

Moral Development

In their early years, children accept and believe in absolute right or wrong. They learn to control their own behavior in order to avoid punishment. Think about the kinds of stories children this age like to hear over and over. Many of their choices are about good and bad behavior and the consequences of behavior choices, even if the characters happen to be talking animals.

Early grade school years are enormously instructive in moral development because the child has moved well beyond the confines of the family unit. Kids soon experience the behaviors of teachers and other students, coaches, the parents of new friends, and many others who present a larger array of values and morals. Some of these behaviors complement and some of them contradict the standards in the home. Sometimes these new influences are positive and sometimes not. There are many new situations to evaluate and many new behaviors for each child to consider and to test.

Around six to seven years old, according to Levine, kids develop a keen interest in what is fair. They constantly analyze family events to make sure that they get a fair share. They can be very picky and precise about the smallest detail, to everyone's annoyance. Their moral development is rather rigid and self-centered. But eventually the idea of fairness extends beyond their own self-interest.[4]

General Development During Ages 4 Through 7

At the beginning of this period, kids are very focused on actual, concrete things. When it comes to interacting with others, they have difficulty putting themselves in another's place or understanding that the other person has a point of view. Initially, they believe that their own point of view is the only one possible. Gradually that concept changes.

Children during this period will begin to initiate sharing as they gain in their capacity to solve problems and to understand cause and effect.

CLIENT EVALUATION

This is a nice example of a behavior that shows us the combination of mental growth and moral development.

They begin to form friendships, and they begin to understand roles and the way in which roles help to define the way people act and the way we are expected to act towards them.

Until the age of about seven, children commonly think that what happens in books, television, or movies is something quite real.

They tell tall tales about themselves and engage in wishful thinking. Adults sometimes misinterpret these as lies, when the child is simply in the process of differentiating what adults consider real and what is pretending.

Children in this age group also experience many fears and anxieties. Quite often these emotions involve imaginary creatures or the dark or being alone and abandoned.

On a lighter topic, humor during this stage revolves around body noises such as burps. They also delight in facial contortions, physical clowning, and slapstick humor.

Physical maturity also increases during these years so that skills and capacities increase and performance improves. Gaining control over coordination and dexterity makes it increasingly possible to do things for themselves and this, in turn, encourages the development of their growing sense of independence.

There are many everyday experiences in the life of your grandchild at this stage which are worthy of attention. Things like learning to dress oneself, helping set the table, making friends, learning religious lessons, taking care of a new puppy, helping with a new sibling, learning to read, beginning ballet or gymnastics, checking out a computer, and so on.

Practice relating each of these activities to a *Three C* value so you can mention those values with ease.

Do keep this small but very important point in mind: because their ability to recall events is limited, you will need to be prepared for *The Birthday Program* with specific questions. Don't be too concerned about exactly when an event or experience actually occurred. Their sense of time does not coincide with an adult's view.

As they begin formal education, schoolwork and academic skills are a significant feature of life. Classroom experiences also include many socialization lessons and the development of interpersonal skills. You might enjoy taking a look at Robert Fulghum's book, *All I Really Need to Know I Learned in Kindergarten,* for suggestions on values that work then and throughout life.[5]

Advising a four-year-old to "mind your manners" may be quite meaningless to the child. It is better to be specific about what to say and do. Give some precise examples. Remind the child to practice saying "please" and "thank you" at school and at home. Or choose other behaviors that begin to demonstrate the self-control and respect for others that come under the general heading of good manners. By the end of this age period, kids should have a good understanding of the meaning and importance of simple, good manners although they won't always remember to use them.

CHAPTER 18. Development in Youth, Ages 8 Through 11

By all accounts, this is a delightful age range. These kids are curious about everything, busy, and generally carefree. They are learning rapidly and seem to have lots to talk about.

Mental Development

Kids in the eight through eleven age range are more able to understand concepts and the relationship of ideas.

Until they are about ten years old, kids generally possess a firm belief, however, that the rules for living come from a higher authority and that, furthermore, they shouldn't be tampered with. Then, around ten or eleven years, they grasp that some rules are subject to interpretation and to change and that they, themselves, can legitimately create those changes. In other words, there are social rules that are arrived at by consensus among members of the group.[1]

You can talk about practical matters like "how things work." They are increasingly capable of thinking through the process that is required to

CLIENT EVALUATION

accomplish everyday tasks. And by the time they reach eleven to twelve they have the capacity to give you a good recap of their school activities in proper sequence.

They still have difficulty, however, comprehending remote situations, the future, and hypothetical matters, although they gradually recognize that death applies to all living things.[2]

Moral Development

Their thinking about right and wrong begins to go through a transition. Judgments, for example, tend to become less rigid or absolute. Youngsters between 8 and 11 years begin to perceive that one can be either good or bad in response to different circumstances. For example, when should we "say what we mean and mean what we say" truthfully (a good value) and when should we employ the admonition to "think before we speak" which reminds us to consider the other person's feelings (another good value). This dilemma is a basic duel between character and civility. Sophistication in making such judgements is what real life is all about. Remember that young people are in a long process of sorting out these matters.

Parents may worry when their child is found cheating in school, but a youngster who feels parental pressure for excellent grades may see it as an expedient response to an impossible demand.[3] That is, it is viewed as a practical rather than a moral issue.

The influence of peers increases in significance. The adults who are guiding them need to be clear on which standards must always be met without fail and which are amenable to interpretation.

These kids also acquire the ability to assign guilt to their own actions during this stage rather than to simply react to the judgment of parents or teachers. Their own conscience begins to provide direction. They also begin to perceive that they won't always be rewarded for good behavior and so they develop more inner motivation. This is a key period for speaking directly about good values, temptations plus self-control and self-regulation.

In this age period and just before puberty, new feelings emerge along with a growing ability to put oneself in another's shoes or to empathize. As they practice the ability to truly understand and appreciate the feelings of others, the meaning of the Golden Rule will have real significance. Use it as a basis for talking about manners, respect, sharing, and other behaviors that you endorse which represent civility. It's a good, simple guide for controlling hurtful impulses towards others.

Children at the end of this age range have feelings which have more depth and power. Because their thinking skills are expanding, they can better evaluate themselves and so they expand their own moral perspective. (Once again we can see how mental and moral development are interrelated and how the combination is shown in behavior.) They may also show a new concern for what is wrong with society's treatment of certain people.[4] This shows mental evaluation of circumstances beyond their own, concerning people they do not know. This social consciousness presents a good opportunity to reinforce feelings of empathy for others which supports our values of civility and citizenship.

General Development During Ages 8 Through 11

During this general stage of development youngsters are rapidly gaining knowledge and skills in socializing and forming friendships. They often have a special friend of the same age and sex, frequently someone who lives nearby. At the same time, interest in the opposite sex and body consciousness begin to emerge during pre-adolescence.

This is the period when kids show an increase in physical ability and coordination. They play games that require coordination and a sequence of motions, such as basketball. Participation in organized sports activities raises issues of relative skills, competitiveness, performance standards, teamwork, and so forth. If your grandchild is a sports enthusiast, use issues of sportsmanship as a way to introduce and discuss values that are meaningful to your grandchild.

A very common experience for boys and girls is learning to ride a two-wheeled bicycle. This is a great opportunity to deal with the process of learning. Think about the character values that are elicited. Bike riding can be a terrific analogy for other things in life that require patience, practice, persistence, and repetition to perfect. But what a reward! The final success results in a glorious sense of freedom and self-sufficiency. Assure your grandchild that she or he can do many other difficult things by remembering that there is a process involved; by taking things slowly,

CLIENT EVALUATION

by thinking the process through, and by practicing over and over you reach your goal.

These youngsters spend much of their time in school and the influence of teachers and peers becomes paramount. The nature of this schooling has a major influence on the child's development. As they approach puberty, peer group pressure and questions of conformity become important to them although they can exercise a new degree of independence within a peer group. The peer group is an arena of separation from adult control. School and peer group experiences provide feedback from others which influences their concept of themselves.

There is a natural tendency to arrange themselves in groups according to various standards and thus to create hierarchies. Think of physical attractiveness or behavior characteristics as examples.

This age period is also the time frame for heroes and hero worship. Youth at the lower end of this age group often select fictional heroes and, for boys, the heroes chosen are frequently violent. It is perfectly natural for this stage. The hero can act in ways that the child cannot although he may have the same feelings. As they grow older, these kids turn to real people as heroes and heroines.

Remember that lots of heroes come from the world of television and your recognition of these characters will enhance your status. Ask them about their heroes, watch a few shows, and use the action, dialog or general theme as discussion topics.

Schoolwork and academic skills continue to be a significant feature of life at this stage. Classroom learning also includes many social matters as well; some are actively discussed as part of the curriculum while others are absorbed without conscious thought or effort.

Personal interests and skill development enrich life and are common during this period. Hobbies and talents are explored. Keeping and caring for pets brings enjoyment and fosters responsibility and commitment.

Learning about money and all that it means is an inevitable and natural element of life at this stage.

CHAPTER 19. Development in Early Adolescence, Ages 12 Through 15

This is the time when everything begins to change and when it becomes harder to make generalizations about the characteristics of all the kids in an age group.

Mental Development

During early adolescence a new mental capacity for more abstract thinking comes into play. However, research indicates that not everyone will gain this ability. It is a kind of reasoning or analysis that lets us speak about concepts without reference to actual, concrete objects. It can be exemplified by, but is not limited to, the capacity to deal with mathematical theory and probability problems or with the principles of physics and chemical interactions. The extent to which adolescents actually do learn these particular subjects is largely dependent on the quality of schooling they receive.

You can see that this new level of mental activity prompts and supports the questioning, the evaluation, and the analysis of everything that so characterizes the early teen years.

We remember that these new mental skills play out in behaviors that adults don't always appreciate. For example, early teens frequently become very self-centered and narcissistic. They acquire a deeper level of understanding of what others are thinking but they all seem to assume that others are thinking about them. They make false assumptions about the content of other minds. They often act very selfishly because they exaggerate their own importance. This also makes them very self-conscious and helps explain why they are so very concerned about their appearance.

Some young teens will argue and debate about everything as they flex their new mental muscles. Their passions are often infused with a new sense of idealism with which they evaluate adult behavior. "Early adolescence is a time of distinguishing oneself from one's parents and they have an easier time describing what they are not, rather than what they are."[1] If you and I can stand back emotionally and recognize that this behavior

CLIENT EVALUATION

means an important new mental muscle is being flexed, then we can respond appropriately.

Moral Development

In the early teen years, youngsters are filled with self-doubt so that the common refrain, "everybody's doing it" represents, for them, a powerful justification for things they want to do. They are especially vulnerable to peer pressure. "Social approval often takes precedence over conscience."[2] During this stage they want, more than anything, to know that they are "normal," and so they automatically want to do what everyone is doing whether it is right or wrong. They may not care to hear about their own unique qualities or attributes nor to stand up for what they know they should do. They look for their strength and security in group membership.

One of the important tasks of this period is learning to control impulses and, even though most teenagers do not engage in sexual intercourse until later adolescence, their attitudes about it are formed in early adolescence.[3] Always remember that their use of sophisticated words about sex does not necessarily denote understanding.

Young teens move from the childhood stage of acquiring moral knowledge, which may or may not include direct religious training, to one of questioning and evaluating the very principles that they have learned. They become more adept at considering particular situations and motives and even less likely to accept absolute rules. They begin to doubt conventional ideas and may become contemptuous of many current moral and social standards.

They can be very perceptive of hypocrisy in what adults say and do. These days, as Coles notes, "many teens have parents who are more interested in psychology than in moral inquiry."[4] According to Coles, this can be confusing, when teenagers are left without guidance or direction. They either drift along or latch onto friends and companions in order to figure out how to behave and why.

These kids are in the process of sorting out and testing the dictates of family and society as they try to solve for themselves the question, "Who am I?" Some of the confusion is shown in the way they dress but much of it is revealed through new levels of personality development, and adults are often advised to regard this experimentation and the variety of styles as symptomatic of growth.[5] That advice is a lot easier for grandparents to manage than it is for parents.

Developmental specialists have determined that young teens don't really forget the values learned in childhood, but they certainly do question and evaluate the application of those values, often against a backdrop of incredibly high ideals.

Finally, they arrive at a more personal, individual point of view concerning what is right and what is wrong.

General Development During Ages 12 Through 15

The time frame during which youngsters enter the physical maturation process that leads to adulthood is difficult to pin down because there are individual variations. Preadolescence is now generally used to describe kids in the ten- to twelve-year age range. At about eleven years for girls and about twelve in boys, a speeding up in growth begins in earnest. In both sexes, this growth spurt is one of the earliest outward signs that puberty has begun.[6]

For some young people there will be no doubt that this transition is underway, for others the change may not begin in an overt fashion. Still, physical development and sexuality are very important matters in early adolescence. Boys seem to lag about two years behind the girls, which is what causes all that embarrassment in junior high school. Growth in girls is generally complete by around age sixteen, whereas boys continue until about eighteen years.[7]

Young teens must adapt not only to their own physical transformation, but also to the rate at which they experience the changes. Given the importance of peer groups and friends, developing either more rapidly or more slowly than the others can be enormously distressing. All kids compare themselves with peers and judge their own situation by comparison. The issues include body size, strength and attractiveness, intellectual abilities, family wealth and status, and clothing choices.[8]

The early adolescent's developing identity and self-concept are intertwined with physical growth. This is a continuous process influenced by parents and peers, the social/educational environment, personal talents and skills, and growth in cognitive development. While some kids appear to "go with the flow" and exhibit rather mild evidence of the changes they experience, others become strangers overnight. They may express their turmoil in a myriad of unexpected ways that can shock and worry family and friends.

Academic expectations and pressures increase, and even though early adolescents have rather vague ideas about the working world, they are often urged to begin vocational considerations. As homework demands increase in frequency and sophistication, computer-literate teens will find opportunities for information, plagiarism, and outright cheating on the screen, often in the privacy of their own bedrooms.

Smoking, alcohol and/or drug use, and sexual behavior are sources of temptation which are influenced by the peer group and the current standards of the youth culture, as well as by parents. Despite their questioning of many adult attitudes and standards, many researchers report that the family and the peer group are dual anchors in the life of an early adolescent. Dare to envision yourself as one of these anchors.

CHAPTER 20. Development in Late Adolescence, Ages 16 Through 19

Growth and development from sixteen years of age to the end of the nineteenth year place a young person on the brink of adulthood. The pursuit of higher education can be a final transition period before the young adult is expected to be fully self-sufficient.

Mental Development

In his later years, Piaget came to believe that the ability to reason hypothetically, logically, and systematically belongs in this age period when thinking tends to be characterized by a sort of intellectual experimentation as teens mentally try out different solutions to a problem.[1] They continue to carry out internal discussions with themselves as they refine their beliefs.

They appear to be more calm and controlled. However, when it comes to risky behavior, which they can intellectually analyze very well, they often lack the capacity to apply this knowledge to themselves. This is gradually moderated as they widen their skills and experiences.

Moral Development

Despite the confusion and intensity of their feelings and the new demands and stresses they experience, idealism and high expectations are common. Spiritual concerns are expressed as they form their own views on such things as the concept of God, their own place in the universe, and whether or not humans have souls and an afterlife. If they have been raised in a particular religion, they usually go through a period of questioning its doctrines.

General Development During Ages 16 Through 19

The last stage of adolescence brings with it a significant point of transition through the acquisition of a driver's license. It is a symbol of adult freedom and independence that is a key event for most teens.

Part-time employment becomes possible. It provides another measure of independence and work supplies money for all of the consumer goods which seem so important.

Much of this period consists of the issues and concerns that predominated in the early teen years—only more so as adolescents exercise their expanding analytical powers.

They are still in the process of self-refinement. At this point they are likely to do an about-face and to distinguish themselves from the crowd that they so wanted to mimic in the previous stage. They become more confident in their own individual characteristics and talents and more capable of forming stable relationships with the opposite sex.

They gradually pay more attention to the future and prepare for college or the work force although some take a detour in the form of pregnancy or the court system. When we add sexually transmitted diseases and substance abuse, we have the major worries of most parents who have teenagers.

CLIENT EVALUATION

How Do Young People View the World?

I consider it advisable to question our own assumptions about the world view that teens hold today, especially because our outlook is tinged with memories of our own experiences. Of course, we think of ourselves as rather "hip" grandparents. Yet we probably don't really appreciate just how modern life affects young people. Although it helps to remember that newspaper headlines of extreme teen behavior don't represent the majority, it would be incorrect to assume that nothing has changed.

As a generation, modern teens are seen as being generally pessimistic. Apparently they believe that they face more serious problems and challenges than any previous group of young people, according to Grace Palladino's research that led to her book called *Teenagers: An American History*.[2]

She wrote, in reference to the mid-1990s, that teens seem to have accepted the idea of themselves as victims of a difficult and violent society. That is a dramatic change from the can-do optimism of the 1950s and 1960s. Many of today's young people think that our country's best days are long gone and that it's much harder to grow up than it used to be. This shocks those of us who look at their material wealth, relative to our own lives at mid-century, and conclude that they have nothing to complain about!

Teens hear stories of just how wonderful things were in the old days from Boomer parents who actually experienced chaotic times. One analyst, according to Palladino, speculates that part of the problem today is that their high expectations of what life *should* be butts up against their lack of tolerance for delaying gratification. They expect to have everything they want and they want it now.[3]

Teens are also inevitably influenced by the generation closest to their own age group, whose members have become part of the adult world. That distinction, for current teens, is held by the cohort called Generation X. This nondescript title refers to the 44.6 million Americans born between 1965 and 1977. They are depicted in the media as being somewhat bland and anonymous in comparison to the huge swath of trend-setting Boomers.[4] Yet they are the most ethnically diverse generation in American history. Nearly 35%, according to the 1990 census, are

Development in Late Adolescence

non-white or Hispanic.[5] A recent research survey, summarized by Margot Hornblower in a 1997 magazine article, helps us understand some of their general group attitudes and opinions.[6]

Generation X has been described as the first generation that grew up with television as their regular babysitter. Now, they are the Internet surfers who are sometimes said to whine a lot. As young adults, they have been perceived as passive and powerless. However, they describe themselves as confident, ambitious, and independent. They believe that older Americans have formed a thoroughly negative evaluation of the members of Generation X which they feel is unfounded.

In a recent magazine report that covered their story, these circumstances were described as contributing factors in the general outlook of their parents and other adults that, in turn, gradually affected the Generation X population: divorce in large numbers, soaring national debt, a bankrupt Social Security system, crack cocaine, Watergate and Iran-Contra, corporate downsizing and layoffs. They have learned to be skeptical of everything. Constant changes in the economic outlook seem to have influenced their collective decision to forget the idea of delaying gratification. As a group they are rather materialistic, a factor that has been attributed to advertising.

The research data showed that 82% like to compete and feel that it improves their performance. Adversity is said to have given them a harder edge. They expect to make their own way because no one is likely to give them anything.

As many as 71% of the members of Generation X believe that it is sometimes necessary to compromise your principles. This percentage is a higher than that of their parents or grandparents. They also are said to relate to situation ethics.

Finally, in the opinion of Rob Owen, they have learned to turn to friends for support and comfort rather than parents or relatives due, in large measure, to the rising divorce rate. Day care played a role in teaching them how to get along with each other. Male/female friendships are often just that, friendship without romance.[7] They are marrying later than any generation in recent memory, and Owen speculates that they may try to reverse the divorce trends and to create more stable family relationships.[8]

CLIENT EVALUATION

This information helps round out the picture we need to keep in mind when we try to see things from their point of view. Generation X has adapted to the society they have inherited by reworking some of the traditional values that we recognize and by making other choices that we dislike. These are the people that teens at the end of the twentieth century tend to mimic.

Use this material in your conversations with them by asking questions. Although you need not agree with their views based on the influences of Generation X, it will be easier to respect their opinions if you know something about the origins of their point of view. Mutual respect is very important if you intend to guide and influence your grandchildren during the teen years.

CHAPTER 21. Research and Record Keeping

These are two very important factors that will contribute to your expertise and success as a consultant.

Research

Those who have had careers dealing with children will have a better store of current knowledge about kids today than will the rest of us. A few trial consultations may show you the advisability of searching out additional background information to fill in the gaps in your knowledge. Likewise, having raised only daughters, for example, means that you should probably pay closer attention to preparations for dealing with grandsons and vice versa. Nor will parenting experience or intuition be a sufficient base for excellence in the performance of your consulting role. But all of them together will provide an excellent head start.

Should the general guidelines presented here on growth and development seem too meager, you may feel curious and become eager to gather more information. Everything that you discover becomes part of your market analysis and will ultimately enhance your performance.

Research and Record Keeping

For example, if you are to be consulting with a child between four and seven years of age, consider that there are many types of preschools with varying philosophies. Kindergarten and grade schools can be different in many ways that will have a direct bearing on the child's daily experiences. Learn as much as you can. Simple things like the time frame of the high school day will tell you whether a teenager has lots of free time. Is that time used for employment or is it completely unstructured?

One of your research tools should be popular literature. A visit to your library will give you lots of information to work with from books and magazines. The teen magazines will give you some clues as to their interests and worries. Also take a look at some of the parenting magazines to discover what is current in child-rearing advice and to appreciate the kinds of information that are relevant to your adult children and their spouses. Although there are a few books that directly address grandparents and more are being produced all the time, the vast majority of written material is still focused on parenting. Despite the fact that this is not our role, it still can be helpful to review some of this literature.

Of course, being modern grandparents we will be making use of information sources on the Internet.

As you work in isolation, searching for information and keeping notes or recording ideas just in case you may want to refer to them later, always remember that you are not working alone. Next door or down the street or in another neighborhood, another city and another state there are more and more people doing just what you are doing for the same reasons.

Record Keeping

Keeping records is an idea that may not seem appealing or even necessary at first, especially if you have only a single grandchild when your consulting process is begun. However, it is being recommended by your franchisor. The volume of material will grow and none of us need to regret a lack of foresight. Keep records from the beginning so that you won't lose track of things. This is especially critical when you are working with more than one grandchild.

A simple file folder per grandchild might be a good place to store articles or notes for later review. If you are in regular contact with a grandchild by phone, E-mail, or "snail mail," add this material to your file and review it prior to your next birthday meeting.

Remember that grandchildren, especially during the early stages, will not be able to recall the timing of events and experiences even though they were terribly important when they occurred. The grandparent must have this information on hand as an option for review and discussion at a later time.

You are also advised to prepare a clear, concise summary of the meeting topics directly following each *Birthday Program* in order to transfer this information into a permanent record called *My Book of Birthdays*. Do this as soon as possible after your consultation.

Another option you might want to consider is the use of a tape recorder during the meeting. Although I have some reservations about this suggestion, it will prevent you from missing anything. An engaging conversation may last longer than you expect and you may lose track of some topics, especially if other events in your life intervene before you can make notes.

SUMMARY

In Part Six, we began to focus directly on our clients. The first step was to review their growth and development so that our expectations of their behavior are in line with their capabilities.

In the next section, Part Seven, we will turn our attention to customer service. This time, the focus moves to our own skills in working with children and teenagers. How can we best deliver our services and be most effective?

A JOB DESCRIPTION FOR GRANDPARENTS (Part 5)

In order to keep their customers happy and to accumulate good references, business consultants need to do as much as they can to understand and appreciate their clients' circumstances and point of view.

Each *Business of Life* client in your family will be an original challenge for your consulting expertise. Possession of a good, basic foundation of information on the general ways that children develop and think will mean that you can give more attention to the immediate experience of talking with each child. Take your work seriously and aim for the creation of a good job reference for yourself.

BUSINESS OF LIFE GRANDPARENT (Part 5)
JOB CONTENT

Possession of a good understanding of the learning capabilities of children at various stages of development will guide the committed grandparent in content and delivery style.

(To be continued.)

PART SEVEN

CUSTOMER SERVICE

There's no doubt about it, *The Birthday Program* must have kid appeal in order to succeed. Customers are the basis for conducting any business whether that business serves the general public, other companies, or particular individuals. Both our good intentions and all of our management skills will be for naught if we fail to honor our grandchildren with excellence in customer service.

Recall my early emphasis on the idea that at least one constant facet of grandparenting should be to focus on the needs of children and teens for wisdom and guidance. Quality customer service is part of our response to those needs.

Good grandparenting may not be rocket science, but it is a real challenge if we keep our standards high. Be assured that there are many ways in which we can stumble and recover in our *Business of Life* process. No single event is an all-or-nothing situation. However, the basics of customer service are crucial to effective consulting, and it is our responsibility to be prepared and self-confident as we begin each birthday meeting. At the heart of *The Birthday Program* is the interaction between grandparent and grandchild, and building that relationship is what customer service is all about.

CHAPTER 22. Customer Relations

One way to look at customer service is to inquire about the relationship values that we must make an effort to demonstrate. We can do a great service to the art of civil discourse if we, as individuals, are models of productive, respectful conversation. If you share the dream of changing America one grandchild at a time, this will be a good place to start.

Truthfulness should be an important cornerstone of our relationships with children so long as it is based on our knowledge of the child's developmental stage. When providing age-appropriate information we shouldn't resort to fantasy or attempt to deflect their curiosity or their fears. Stick to the point and deal with the issue at hand.

Acknowledge your grandchild's feelings, treat them as genuine, and don't attempt to avoid them or deny their existence. Can you hear some bad examples of what I'm referring to? "Oh, you're not afraid of that little dog, are you?" or "How can you possibly feel sad when you have such a wonderful life?" or "What do you mean—you hate your mother?" These are samples of ordinary human reactions to ordinary situations. Children experience all of the basic emotions that grown-up people experience. Let's not rush to pretend that they never feel afraid, miserable, or angry.

If you accept your grandchildren as they truly are, they will come to you voluntarily when they are in need of information or help. In contrast, if you have discouraged openness or contradicted their feelings, they may simply avoid sharing their problems with you in the future.[1]

Consistent truthfulness about what you know and believe, plus your honesty about admitting it when you don't have a ready answer, helps build trust. Trust is a wonderful bonding agent. Give your client that kind of confidence in your relationship.

The ability to maintain trust and confidence depends on privacy. Your *Birthday Program* meetings must be private events, especially with older children and teenagers. Don't take privacy lightly because you are dealing with a young person. It will be to your advantage to give them this kind of assurance well before you are conversing with a teenager. Privacy matters.

Privacy implies but does not ensure confidentiality. It is my belief that confidentiality is a basic necessity for *Business of Life* grandparenting. There should be no exception for nosy parents or siblings. It is particularly important during preteen and teen years, but it would be wise to begin in confidence and maintain that confidence rather than try to change course later. If you violate this commitment to teenagers who have come to have faith and trust in the security of your conversations, then your relationship may be irreparable.

What If I Encounter Real Trouble?

In my opinion, there is only one circumstance which calls for a re-evaluation of our pledge of confidentiality.

You may be torn and indecisive about some of the problems that a trusting teenager may want to reveal to you. React immediately if you hear something that prompts you to seriously worry about suicide. Suicide may be just a topic of some curiosity and interest and may not be personal. Perhaps a news story or a school rumor will prompt a teen to talk about the subject. But sometimes things that adults consider minor are enough to tip the balance for a teenager who may see the act as a solution to insurmountable problems. The motivation may seem incredibly minor from an adult's point of view.

Specialists conclude that many adolescents reach a point of utter despair.[2] This sometimes happens when a series of setbacks

CUSTOMER SERVICE

comes in quick succession. The future looks like more of the same and it becomes overwhelming in the teen's mind. Statistics also show that more girls make suicide attempts, but that more boys actually succeed.

Important clues may come in comments such as, "I can't take it anymore" or "I want to die," or the child may begin giving away personal items. Sometimes, at this point, the youngster's spirits rise and they seem happier. This may be relief at having found a solution—the wrong one, of course, but adults frequently misinterpret this change in attitude, assume that the crisis has passed, and relax.[3]

This subject can be a tricky one as teens often make exaggerated claims and predictions. We don't want to become knee-jerk alarmists. However, the old adage "better safe than sorry" should be our slogan in this decision-making dilemma. Should I be faced with this situation, I would ask the child's parents about what they have observed in the child's recent behavior and express my concerns. I would also apologize to my grandchild for breaking my commitment to confidentiality and explain my reason for doing so.

According to historical data, some 10,000 teens will succeed in killing themselves every year and another 400,000 will try.[4] I would like to think that *Business of Life* grandparenting will give our grandchildren an outlet to talk openly and provide them with enough continuous support and guidance that such a decision would never occur to them.

Now you may feel strongly about your responsibility to alert parents or others to additional problem behaviors, and it may be wise to do so. First, give yourself a little time to consider the situation and how best to proceed. I would also talk again with the teenager to make sure I understood and to tell her or him that I felt it necessary to break confidence because I deeply believed it to be in their best interests to do so.

My advice is NOT that of a professional. I am only describing what my own reactions would be, as a concerned grandparent, under some very serious circumstances. Your own judgment should be paramount in such a situation.

How Can I Build Good Relationships with My Grandchildren?

The creation of a relationship that can be sustained is the first responsibility of a good consultant. A good relationship starts with knowledge of our grandchildren in depth and in detail. We should discover what they expect of life and what they experience in living it.

Consultants should anticipate the development of a long-term relationship and we should do our part by showing respect, learning to listen attentively, and knowing how to respond appropriately.[5] Let's delve into each of these elements in turn.

Respect

Here is a good basic principle as expressed by Dick Schaff in his book on customer service. "The quality of long-term service depends less on what we try to control and more on what we do in harmony with others."[6] Harmony implies respect. Respect is a basic value that grandparents must exemplify during *Birthday Program* meetings and in all of our dealings with our grandchildren.

How do we act when we show our respect for another person? Read IMAGINE: Exercise Number Five and carry your thoughts with you as you return to the text.

**IMAGINE
Exercise
Number Five**

Respect

Imagine hosting a dinner for your business associate, an executive, and her husband. The table is spread with a white linen cloth and your finest china and crystal. Everyone has just been seated.

CUSTOMER SERVICE

As you propose a toast, your male guest reaches for his glass, bumps it, and spills red wine all over the table.

WORKSHEET for IMAGINE: Exercise Number Five

Write down your first words in response to this incident just as you would say them on the spot.

_____
_____
_____
_____
_____
_____
_____
_____

Second, make some quick notes of the actions you would take.

_____
_____
_____
_____
_____
_____

I trust that between you and your spouse, one of you would move swiftly to take up the cloth while the other made light of the matter and refilled the guest's wine glass. Neither of you would think to berate your guest for being clumsy or to shame him in any way. There would be no effort to exacerbate his embarrassment.

This response demonstrates more than good manners on the part of the hosts. It shows respect for your guest and confidence in his integrity. It reveals the hosts' assumption that accidents happen and their conviction that this was the explanation for the spilled wine.

Children likewise deserve this same kind of respect, this assumption on our part of their basic goodness and their desire to behave properly even as they are learning the rules. Children are not possessions. They are particular individuals, entrusted to the care and guidance of adults, who should treat them with the same respect and dignity that we show any other guests in our home.

Practice thinking of your grandchildren as honored guests in your life.

The Art of Listening

When it comes to interacting with others, a great deal has been written on the art of listening. For a consultant, this art is crucial. There are enormous benefits to be gained from being able to set aside our own self-centered outlook and our own impulses and tendencies to control the conversation. While we want to guide the flow, we also want to dismiss artificial rigidity. By simply listening, we open the way for the expression of empathy. Children, like adults, know when we are really listening and paying attention to their point of view.

It is also important that we listen with respect, maintain confidentiality, keep an open mind, and accept the child's feelings. From a child's point of view, feeling accepted despite mistakes and faults is very comforting, especially when we also express faith in the youngster's ability to resolve problems, to learn, and to grow.[7]

In the perennially popular book, *How To Win Friends and Influence People*, Dale Carnegie advised that we could make more friends and make them faster if we took a real interest in other people instead of talking about ourselves when we meet someone new.[8] He knew that, all too often, we are our own favorite subjects and we love to talk about ourselves. Take his advice and practice substituting listening for talking.

But When Do I Talk About My Life?

As you transfer this advice to your consulting role, remember that the purpose of *Business of Life* conversations is not to give you a chance to tell your story. No doubt you have an interesting story to tell. Keep it between the covers of the separate scrapbook or journal that you are preparing to share with your grandchildren on other occasions.

The *Business of Life* Job Description calls for focusing on your grandchild's life in progress. It's all right to comment on a feeling that you shared at the youngster's age or an experience you had in common. Still, resist the urge to go into detail. Practice self-restraint and redirect your attention to your grandchild. We are encouraged by many knowledgeable specialists to show genuine interest in the other person, adult or child, and that is *not* the same as waiting patiently for *our* turn to talk.

This clever reminder is so perfect that I hope you will commit it to memory as I have.

Reminder!

The more you listen, the more they hear you.

Carnegie knew that the secret to being a good conversationalist is to *listen!* Listen and encourage others to talk about themselves. As capable consultants, we now know that encouragement takes the form of managerial skills by asking open-ended questions, using probing questions, and restating to confirm our understanding. We're going to keep those clients talking.

People in a true business setting are cautioned to control their own impulsive reactions to comments they hear from clients. The best managers and consultants are those who have learned not to rush to judgment. They take a deep breath and think first before they respond.[9] This is a key point for grandparenting. Take a deep breath and think before you speak. Kids are quite capable of provocative outbursts. Their vocabulary is often much more adult than we might expect and it can be quite shocking. Expect that and practice a simple, all-purpose response in your own mind. Remember that the youngster's use of an adult word doesn't necessarily signify an understanding of its meaning. You are *not* being advised to ignore awful words. You are being advised to control and organize your response.

Here's another modern twist to the art of listening that I find appealing. Proactive listening has been recommended by Kim Krisco in place of reactive listening. The proactive style means that you listen *for* certain things. Things like compassion, wisdom, or anything that you would be glad to hear, like an example of a good value or behavior.[10] This is more than accentuating the positive, which is good in itself. It takes fine-tuning. It reflects our grandparenting goal of interpreting what we hear as representative of *The Three C's.*

Practice listening proactively. Listen for things that represent *character, civility,* and *citizenship* and comment on them at once. You might want to make use of the restatement technique to endorse the child's behavior. Take the opportunity to introduce the appropriate adult word as you compliment the behavior. Encourage your grandchild to make that attitude a habit.

Proactive listening is really the underlying point of the birthday consultations. By skillful questioning and attentive listening, you should be able to glean, from your grandchild's experiences, the material that you need to discuss good values. Why? Because values are exemplified in that child's thoughts, attitudes, and responses to the regular events of his or her life. Our job is to pay attention to those events with a bias towards the value-based content and to build that focus into the conversation.

What Good Can Come from Listening?

How often have you heard the lament, "No one ever listens to me"? You've probably said or thought as much yourself at one time or another. Remember that being listened to and understood is a fundamental human need. Keep this wonderful, old Romanian proverb in mind: "Men are born with two ears and one tongue in order that they may listen twice as much as they talk."[11] This is an open invitation for good grandparenting. Whenever you hear yourself doing too much talking or notice that your grandchild's attention has begun to wander, ask a question, and listen proactively.

Besides filling a basic need, listening does other good things. In his book, *How to Influence Children*, Charles E. Schaefer suggests that listening can actually help promote self-esteem because a child will come to believe that he is *worth* listening to and that his ideas and concerns have value. That's a satisfying reason for being a good listener. Listening also strengthens the child's ability to solve her own problems when the grandparent is non-judgmental and asks questions that support the child's ability to think things through.[12]

Try this tactic every now and then. Even if you are asked a question, you can toss it right back by asking, "What do you think about that?" or "What does it mean to you?" and then prepare to listen carefully. This technique can help you grasp what the youngster has in mind and you may be surprised to realize that you expected something quite different. Had you answered, instead of tossing the question back, you would have completely missed the point! This technique is especially helpful when you are asked a question that takes your breath away. You know, such as when you are asked blunt questions about sex or death or similar major topics that you could spend a lot of time trying to explain thoroughly in order to do justice to the issue. Bouncing the question back will buy you some time and let you take direction from your grandchild. Sometimes the information that they really want is very simple.

The skilled listener is not expected to be silent throughout these conversations. In fact, your assignment is to provide wise counsel and to make comments that will be remembered. Natural conversation does not provide a predetermined opportunity to do so in the way that a lecture might. Do practice simple, concise messages and then ask a question to determine whether your listener actually heard what you meant to convey.

It might be fun to revisit some of the aphorisms that were certainly common in my young life and probably in yours, as well. These short and memorable little sayings can pack quite a punch. More often than not, they summarize values and good ways to behave. You can say a lot with few words. A list of some of the pertinent choices can be found in Chapter 27.

Why Is Our Expertise So Important?

Unfortunately, many parents don't have time to listen and others may not be good at it. Schaefer reminds us that parents fill the role of disciplinarians and as such, they have a tendency to resort to lecturing, scolding, offering solutions, and relating their own personal experiences. This means that children and teenagers are rather likely to be the focus of parental talking instead of parental listening.[13] Even though they may want and need to talk to their parents, kids can easily be put off by this confrontational habit.

How Can We Be Effective When Dealing with Teenagers?

Talking with teens can seem to be a daunting task. First, many specialists on the teen years recognize that parents are themselves in a stressful period of life. Midlife is a time when many are dealing

CUSTOMER SERVICE

with various disappointments such as a job loss or the need for additional education for advancement. There may be a divorce or the stresses of dual careers or a serious illness in the family. These problems can drain their energy and distract their attention.

Parents also begin to experience some of the physical changes of middle adulthood. As their youth and vigor and sense of endless possibilities in life begin to decrease somewhat, their teenage offspring are on the brink of opportunities with their full potential yet to be realized. This can make for a difficult mix of changes and needs on the part of both generations living in the same house. As a result, the parents' capacity to really listen may be diminished. Most teens would probably prefer to be able to talk with a parent in most circumstances. However, there are also times when another adult can be especially helpful. Why?

Judy Blume, who has written many books for teens, receives endless letters from them asking for help, guidance, or just a listening ear. In her book, *Letters to Judy: What Your Teens Wish They Could Tell You*, she speculates that sometimes it is easier for them to confide in her because she won't be there to confront them at the breakfast table the next morning. She is someone they have come to trust through her writing, someone who won't be tempted to use this personal information against them. She is even forthright about the fact that her own children sometimes turned to other adults for advice.[14]

This person so coveted by teens, who is calm and willing to listen, who is close enough yet somewhat removed from their daily lives, could very well be a grandparent. I recommend that you read or skim Blume's book in order to jog your memory and freshen your sensitivity to the things that normal teens want to know about.

It's my understanding that most of the youngsters who have written to Judy Blume about their problems have been girls. If you're a grandmother, it's probably comfortable and natural to imagine yourself talking easily with granddaughters. But what about the boys?

William Pollack, a clinical psychologist, is the author of *Real Boys*. In his book, he makes a telling point regarding one of our collective expectations about the behavior of boys. Boys in our society aren't supposed to talk about their feelings. They get this message early and they understand the rule. Consequently, they are usually without the ongoing counsel of a concerned adult during their formative years. They know that they are supposed to be strong and to tough things out. Yes, they are allowed and encouraged to ask for useful information about how things work, for example. But it's the girls, of course, who are routinely expected to talk about their feelings.[15]

Will you grandfathers be willing and able to step into the breach? Or you grandmothers? This is an issue that deserves our careful attention. Do some reading and some thinking about this situation because a change in this cultural pattern will require an adjustment in our own attitudes and expectations. Consider the importance of male and female friends to Generation Xers. In the younger generations, a natural discussion of feelings is being highlighted. This may be an area of unspoken and unmet need for our grandsons.

Remember the rebelliousness and the curiosity that teens have about everything? Do you appreciate the dire consequences that surround some of today's risky choices that teens face? There are serious issues involved here. Sometimes it doesn't seem possible to talk about them calmly, let alone just to listen! Expect to be subjected to some serious complaining now and then or to an opening that could lead to an angry confrontation unless you handle it with finesse. Teenagers like to test our resolve and gauge our intentions now and then. Sometimes the things they want to know about are philosophical; often they are about relationships. Sometimes they may even seem silly when we compare them to our own experiences or to the problems that we know of. Just remind yourself that you're not the parent this time and relax.

Spend some time reminiscing on your own so that you can get in touch with the teenager you used to be. We may have acted grown up then, but we didn't always feel that way! Think about the universal concerns that all teens have, at one time or another. Making the effort to be open and available for your teenaged grandchildren, as well as to be involved with them through *The Birthday Program*, will be well worth it in the long run and listening with respect is a necessity.

The Art of Talking

This should be a snap. But, in reality, talking is also a skill that deserves thoughtful consideration. We already have the fundamentals based on the types and uses of several styles of questioning. Let's review some other elements of this art.

How Do I Say What Needs to Be Said?

Writing for parents in the mid-sixties, Dr. Haim Ginott pointed to the results that can be gained by skillful and caring conversations. He wrote that we are all most effective in providing feedback when we state our own feelings and thoughts without attacking the other person's personality and dignity. Notice that we aren't consulting to show how smart we are or to win as though it were a competition. So, be prepared to show yourself, nonverbally and verbally, during your consultations, without using words or gestures as weapons.

Highlight Dr. Ginott's recommendation in your memory banks. State your own feelings and thoughts without attacking, even though your feelings may be intense at first. Grandparents should make the effort to listen and respond with sensitivity.

Ginott believed that such a sympathetic atmosphere models fairness, consideration, and civility, which are good values to demonstrate.[16] Grandparents should be able to show by example that values are not to be reserved for use only when they happen to be convenient.

The preferred approach with teens is an easygoing one. They may avoid the issue they really want to talk about while they size up your general attitude and your receptivity. A too quick and slick judgment from Granddad can bring an abrupt halt to any possibility for serious interaction, and you may never know what you missed. Take your time, get your bearings, listen, and ask for clarification before you get involved.

Conversation skills are especially important when working with teens. Practice leading questions or state your concerns. For example: "What do you know about this?" "How do you feel when it comes to _____?" "Do you know what might happen if you do?" "I remember wanting to try that. I was curious and scared at the same time." "How do you feel about it?" "Do they teach you about this at school?" "Does it seem like everyone else is?" "What do you think about it?" "This subject worries me and I'm curious about your view." "I get angry when I think about_____, so I have to slow myself down and evaluate it carefully." "What are the good points and what are the bad points here?" "Maybe this could affect your future." "Gee, I never thought about that; let me see what I can find out." And so forth.

You won't be able to solve everything for them, nor will any of us, and we shouldn't expect to. But we can show concern and caring. Try complimenting your teenager in advance by stating your expectations about the young person's ability to make good decisions. Remind them that you are available any time they need you.

All Right, But What Are the Real Secrets?

Teens like to think that they are quite grown up and so they seem to respond well when we treat them as young adults. When it comes to talking with teens, here is my own personal best suggestion. Ask them for advice. Yes, that's right. Nothing signals your faith in their developing maturity so much as to have you seek information *from* them.

Ask for their opinions, their thoughts, their concerns, and their evaluation. Ask for their help with your computer problems. Ask them what they think the future will be like.

My second best suggestion is that you deal with teenagers just as you would with your own adult friends. You agree to disagree on some points with your spouse and friends, don't you? This is a perfectly valid outcome when talking with teens and it will be inevitable some of the time. Have you also experienced an adult conversation about something controversial only to have a friend say later that your comments prompted him to rethink his position? This also happens with teens although they may not admit it directly.

A difference of opinion, respectfully discussed, can later turn into a coming together of your mutual beliefs. Consulting is always a process. Use this dialogue to steer, to challenge, to focus, and to inquire about the whole range of concerns that mark a teen's development. Be on the ball; be ahead of her game. Always express your confidence in her ability to work things out just as you would give a vote of confidence to a friend.

You may be thinking that all this sounds very nice while wondering about those times when tough talk is necessary. Sometimes it isn't smart or helpful to be calm and polite. Sometimes being direct and blunt is just spontaneous. When it's genuine and heartfelt, it has its place. I was reminded of this fact by a full-page newspaper advertisement recently placed by a national organization fighting drug use by children. The text advocated intervention by grandparents in helping prevent experimentation, with the idea that grandparents don't beat around the bush. Instead, they ask direct, point-blank questions that may be embarrassing. This approach can be forceful without being demeaning or accusatory yet the method, even with drugs as the topic, is still based on asking questions rather than scolding or lecturing. Grandfather's style when conversing with Caitlin about taking care of her glasses was a simple, realistic version of the direct approach.

How Do I Express Empathy?

Today, the caring word of choice is empathy. It means that we try to identify with and understand another's feelings, situation, or motives. Even though many of us come from generations when talking about your feelings wasn't common, this is something we can learn to become comfortable with. When applied to grandparenting, it means that we must try to see and feel things from our grandchild's point of view.[17] We try to put ourselves in their shoes, and this is where honest memories about your own youth can serve you well by helping you recall your own feelings.

Empathy includes helping a preteen, for example, sort out feelings, but it rules out directly telling them what to feel. Neither does it give us the right to contradict them when they tell us what their feelings are. Empathy suggests that we listen and accept what we hear even when the person we're listening to feels hurt, frightened, or angry. Allow them to express the bad as well as the good. No sugar coatings, please.

Empathy requires use of good conversation skills. It is based on the sense of inherent human equality and respect that we have explored. Neither love and caring nor good intentions will, by themselves, bring about the results that can come from expressions of empathy.

Some examples of empathetic comments from authors Leland and Bailey would be:

- "I can see why you feel that way."
- "I see what you mean."
- "That must be very upsetting."
- "I understand how frustrating that must be."[18]

The responsibility for every grandparent is to exemplify the values that we intend to impart to our grandchildren. They are the basics of good customer/client service.

CONSULTANT VALUES FOR RELATIONSHIP BUILDING

Empathy plus Honesty,
especially when you don't have the answer, result in
Trust and Confidence.

> Privacy plus Confidentiality strengthen
> Trust and Confidence.
>
> Respect plus Listening proactively
> plus Conversation skills
> support and promote good grandparent/
> grandchild relationships.

This Sounds Like All Talk and No Action

There are a few experts whose recommendations don't stop at good advice for listening and responding. Krisco encourages leaders, mentors, and coaches to conclude most conversations by encouraging action. "By using requests, eliciting promises or commitments, [grandparents] can also initiate activities and behaviors in order to put things in motion that can transform possibilities into realities."[19] By following up at a later date with inquiries into the status of the action that was planned, you have the opportunity to continue to support the mastery of the lesson. Ask probing questions. Continue to provide encouragement. Show enthusiasm for the effort, but please don't burden the youngster with demands for something that you define as perfection. Relax and let life happen.

This leads us directly to the matter of praise and criticism. Now everyone knows intuitively that criticism is about to be condemned and praise to be endorsed. Read on.

CHAPTER 23. Praise and Criticism

Motivating children by praising them has become nearly as popular among Americans as the blame game. There must be something to it. I wonder what you remember in terms of being praised as a child. What was your experience with criticism? Lets explore these emotion-packed opposites so that each of us can come to terms with them.

Praise

Many specialists in child development have looked closely at the use of praise. Research has shown the relationship between praise, self-esteem, and a child's actual behavior really is not as simple as we tend to think it is. For example, excessive praise for a poor performance can be disturbing to a child. Kids, even young ones, get credit for being pretty savvy about whether or not they and others actually deserve praise.

In *Your School-Age Child,* Kutner reports on an experiment in which youngsters watched a video of a teacher praising one child for solving arithmetic problems while simply commenting to another child that he had done a good job on the problems. Next, the kids watching the video were asked which of the kids doing the math problems was less smart. Most of them selected the child who was praised. Why? Because they concluded that the teacher didn't think very highly of that student. Praise was interpreted as a substitute for competence, and so they viewed it as a sign of inferiority in the child who received it.[1] If a youngster is doing just fine, she expects a response from the teacher that is calm and little more than a point of recognition. It is an acknowledgement that implies, "I knew you could."

Just how do you feel about false flattery? Surely, you have had the experience of receiving it. Does it endear the flatterer to you? Teachers, coaches, and many adults seem to think that a child who gives a poor showing will feel better if the effort is rewarded with enthusiasm. Using his own childhood experiences with sports, Kutner points out that kids reach the same negative conclusion when they see a poor player being highly praised. Unfortunately for the child, this undeserved attention clearly separates him or her from the group and highlights the inferiority.[2]

The author of *Punished by Rewards,* Alfie Kohn, asks the reasons that we make use of praise. What is it that we are trying to do? He predicts that most adults would respond with these general ideas.

CUSTOMER SERVICE

We are trying:

- to enhance performance,
- to promote appropriate behavior or positive values,
- to help give the individual good feelings.[3]

Does praise actually produce these results? Unfortunately, the answer is likely to be negative because praise actually tends to thwart our good intentions. The result may be quite the opposite of our initial expectations.

Praise may actually be a problem because:

- it often signals low ability,
- it makes people feel pressured,
- it invites a low-risk strategy to avoid failure,
- it can reduce interest in the task itself.[4]

Even if your first reaction is to deny these possibilities, they are serious enough that each of us should make an effort to think carefully about them. For grandparents, the inclination to gush with praise seems almost natural. The absence of any need for critical appraisal is often cited as one of the features that makes grandparenting so delightful.

It's a false premise, I think, because we certainly object when our grandchildren are naughty, belligerent, or strenuously boastful. If we are going to make use of modern advances in how best to work with other people, especially young people, we need to stop and take note of the use of praise.

According to Kohn, if a child learns to respond appropriately only when praise is expected, it can reduce the likelihood of good behavior when no one is around to praise it. And no matter the current fashion in "pop" psychology, effusive praise does not produce a healthy self-concept. We simply don't become confident in ourselves just because someone says nice things to us.[5]

What is a grandparent, especially one who wants to endorse admirable performance, to do about the use of praise? There is lots of good advice on this score from many sources.

Giving positive feedback does not require us to offer praise at all. Specific, straightforward words are just fine and are without damaging consequences. An even tone of voice and a relaxed facial expression should support the delivery of the message.

Think about an airplane made from small blocks by your grandchild. If you are surprised and pleased with his or her accomplishment, let it show; but don't stop there. Cast an appraising eye and mention the careful work that was necessary. Ask if the youngster created the design and comment on the skill required whether it was copied or original. Compliment the patience that was necessary. Inquire about the child's evaluation of the outcome. This conversation is more likely to leave the block-builder self-satisfied and feeling good about her or his capabilities because Grampa recognized what it took to produce the creation. In other words, the work, the planning, and the effort that were involved have been acknowledged and supported. Those things are more real and more satisfying than to receive nothing more than a look of astonishment and delight.

This style of honest appraisal and feedback is generally appropriate whether we are commending performance or correcting it. Adults are advised to find ways to talk with children so as to encourage them without falling into the easy trap of throwing out general praise or doing things for kids when we really want them to learn how to do things on their own. It isn't necessary to wring all emotion out of these situations. Just be sure that your reaction is reasonable and appropriate.

Train yourself to think "compliment" instead of praise. To compliment means to remark favorably on something *specific*. Rather than saying, "My, what a wonderful girl you are. You're just so smart," instead say, "I can see that you took your time and worked carefully on those math problems." In the latter case, you compliment a good performance. If you want to really emphasize your view, you could note that the questions were difficult. This gives extra credit to the youngster for being tenacious and for applying

CUSTOMER SERVICE

the lessons learned in class to her homework. This kind of compliment is meaningful. It feels good and it feels right because it is unlikely that every problem was solved correctly on the first effort. This dedication to trial and error is simply the truth about succeeding at any endeavor. We humans must try and learn and practice until we finally get it (whatever it is) right.

Let's see how this topic was handled recently in Sunshine City, USA.

A CONSULTATION WITH NATALIE

Setting: A bedroom that is clearly inhabited by a tomboy.

Participants: Natalie, who will be nine years old in a few days, and Grandmother, who never does have another birthday.

The occasion: It is near the end of summer and vacation time will soon be over. Natalie's birthday, which falls in the middle of the first week of school, is being celebrated a few days early. A regular *Business of Life* consultation is already underway. As we pick up the conversation, Grandmother has found the opening she needs to bring up another topic.

Action: Natalie picks up a softball, tosses it up, then catches it in her mitt.

Grandmother: "Summer's almost gone. How do you feel about going back to school?"

Natalie: "I am READY." (She makes this announcement with gusto.)

Grandmother: "I guess that means you're eager to look through your new books."

Natalie: "Uh huh. They're gonna be TOTALLY cool."

Grandmother (chuckling): "My goodness. You should rub some of that enthusiasm off on your sister." She pauses. "Your mom told me that you scored pretty high on those I.Q. tests they gave all of you last spring. Sounds to me as though you'll be in some advanced classes this year. Am I right?"

Natalie: "Yeah." (She is quiet for a few moments.) "Me and all the other smart kids."

Grandmother: "Tell me something. What does being really smart mean?"

Natalie: "It's easy to do stuff."

Grandmother: "Is that so? What about studying, then? Do you smart kids need to bother with it?"

Natalie (frowning in concentration): "Well, I guess so ... maybe not as much as the other kids, you know? It's all easy for us."

Grandmother: "Honey, I think you may be surprised when you get back in class." (She nabs the softball and tosses it from hand to hand.) "Here's a question for you. Do smart kids ever make mistakes?"

Natalie: "Well, yeah. I mean I do . . . sometimes."

Grandmother: "Remember that and never be worried about making mistakes or experimenting or thinking hard or doing more homework. That's what REALLY intelligent people do. I've always been happy to see that you enjoy studying and discovering new ideas. It's exciting, isn't it?" (Natalie nods and smiles.) "How do you feel after you've worked and struggled to figure something out and you finally understand?"

Natalie (glowing, leans over, and whispers confidentially): "We're two smart girls, aren't we, Gramma?"

This conversation continued for a short while on other topics.

How would you critique Grandmother's performance in this dialogue? It appears that she almost lapsed into lecturing before she caught herself and asked a closed-ended question. Would you make more use of open-ended or probing questions in this situation? Would you have used a larger assortment of preferred customer service techniques? There was an opportunity to express empathy, wasn't there? Grandmother either missed it or ignored it. On the other hand, maybe you suspect that there are times when it's necessary and appropriate to state your case right up front. When it comes right down to it, there is no absolute right or wrong in these situations unless we do nothing but lecture.

CUSTOMER SERVICE

It is true that Grandmother was particularly concerned about this topic due, in part, to a newspaper article that she had read only a few days before this visit. The article referred to a recent study that showed the negative effects of praising intelligence in children and the very positive results of praising their efforts. It's likely, too, that she is anticipating the impact of puberty on Natalie and the looming social pressure to be popular rather than smart.

In retrospect, Grandmother decided that she had made a good beginning in her attempt to separate (in Natalie's mind) direct praise for innate intelligence from support for the skills and rewards of trial and error. Later, Grandfather would also pick up on the idea of "tools for learning" in his endorsement of the rewards of individual effort. Of course, these ideas will be shared with each grandchild in turn. However, in this case it has added significance because Natalie has been publicly identified as naturally superior in mental capacity.

The evidence is thoroughly convincing. Compliments for specific actions recognize the youngster's ability to make use of the process of achievement. That is the source of self-confidence and self-esteem. Praise that is pure adoration does not reinforce the child's capabilities in any meaningful way.

Here then is a summary of the key points to keep in mind about the use of praise:

- Don't praise people, only what people do.
- Make praise as specific as possible.
- Avoid phony praise.
- Avoid praise that sets up a competition.[6]

As *Business of Life* grandparents, it is important to remember that no thought is necessary when we offer praise. It takes skill, care, and attention to encourage people in such a way that they remain interested in what they are doing without feeling controlled. Resist the urge to take over and do things or solve problems for them. Show your pleasure and your interest in their accomplishments by giving your grandchildren thoughtful compliments.

Rewards

The authors of *20 Teachable Virtues* actually warn parents against the use of tangible rewards based on their belief that children who are given stickers, candy, toys, or other things for doing what they are expected to do don't internalize the lesson. They learn to perform only for a prize. Then they begin to expect that rewards always follow good behavior. This is not at all what we grandparents would want to accomplish.[7]

Rewards have also been described as detriments because they offer a specific but false incentive for performing. They change the way we perform and they change the attitude we take toward the activity. The whole point of immediate rewards is to control people's behavior, according to Kohn.[8] Sure, everyone uses rewards occasionally when caught in a pinch, but the habitual use of rewards is quite another matter. In fact, research has shown that unexpected rewards are much less destructive than those kids are told about ahead of time.[9] I think that's an important distinction and a point for grandparents, especially, to keep in mind. A surprise treat to commemorate an accomplishment can be a great delight to the giver as well as the receiver. Still, don't let it become a pattern.

Think of a king of long ago, perhaps during the early middle ages. He would have been all-powerful and able to dole out estates and privileges as he chose. Think of the palace intrigue and the dastardly deeds committed as competitors vied for recognition and enrichment. That would have been just the environment for the use of rewards, a situation where there was a great power imbalance and only one person who sat in judgment of what the contenders did and how well they performed.

This kingdom gives us a pretty good example of what children experience when adults make use of rewards on a regular basis. Recognize that our king can trust no one. There is no real friendship or partnership in the kingdom. Everyone has ulterior motives. There is little incentive for doing altruistic deeds or pursuing noble causes. No one will risk angering the king by taking any initiative. What a sorry situation this is when we transpose it to modern times and impose it upon children.

Rewards can be thought of as extrinsic motivators or something that is provided by others instead of coming from within. Where no reward is promised, a compliment on the child's performance allows him to accept within himself—that is, intrinsically—personal satisfaction in the achievement. This child has a much better chance of learning to set personal goals, in any area of life, in order to derive that sense of personal pleasure that comes with trying and improving step by step. Of course this person may delight in occasional extrinsic rewards, but they are rarely the prime motivators.

As a method of forming character and encouraging civil behavior and meeting the demands of citizenship, rewards are sorry substitutes for training and guidance. *The Three C's* thrive when there is intrinsic motivation, when a grandchild feels the desire to do things for the internal satisfaction or the joy of doing them. Such intrinsic motivation is a powerful force and it brings out the best in us. A too-frequent use of rewards can be counterproductive when we seek behavior based on values and morals. Why? Because, in the worst case, if a child is trained only to perform for rewards then performance will fall off quickly unless the rewards escalate and any means whatsoever can be used to justify their acquisition including lying, cheating, or stealing. A sense of entitlement may be created.

Clearly, the thoughtless doling out of rewards is not a useful technique for our customer service repertoire, and in our efforts to be effective consultants, we should curb this tendency not only during *The Birthday Program*, but also in our routine interaction with our grandchildren.

Criticism

The potential problems caused by too frequent use of rewards meet their match in the use of criticism. Dale Carnegie believed that criticism and condemnation are dreadful ways to try to change behavior whether they are directed towards children or adults. And yet, we adults persist in believing that we're actually being helpful when we point out errors.[10]

Carnegie passionately believed that it is a crime to damage another's dignity—children included.[11] Instead of attacking, he advocated techniques which will let the other person save face.

For example, he gave a wonderfully simple solution to the question of how to get the results we want without resorting to direct disapproval. The situation he used was that of a parent who felt the need to criticize his son's report card. Carnegie knew that most of us would begin by praising the good grades, then we would say *but*, and criticize the poor marks. Any child would feel good in the beginning. However, after hearing *but*, things change. In a flash, the youngster would begin to question the sincerity of the praise. That original compliment now feels like a way to soften the blow that's coming rather than a sincere expression. That *but* ruins everything that preceded it and Carnegie believed that it was unlikely to change the youngster's attitude.[12]

What would be a better alternative? Change the word *but* to *and*, Carnegie advised. It's as simple as that. After complimenting the good grades say, " . . . and I know that you will continue your hard work so that all of these grades will be good on your next report card." That not only makes the compliment real, it also describes what we want the child to do next. It is clear to me that this simple technique is one that a wise consultant would want to put into practice.

Using other examples, Carnegie wanted to show that so much of what passes for teaching, coaching, or mentoring only highlights what kids are not to do rather than identifying what is to be done.[13] Don't let yourself fall into that trap.

Think about the following statement carefully. When we criticize, it's as though we imagine that kids really know how to do the right thing in any situation and are just willfully ignoring it. After reviewing child growth and development, we know this to be an absurd premise.

Let's use a grandparenting example involving younger children when they visit at your house. I believe that you and your spouse have every right to set the rules for their behavior in your home. How can it be done most effectively?

Sit down with your grandchild soon after his or her arrival and tell them that this house has rules. Note that these are not rules that *you* are imposing, they belong to the house. Everyone should obey them, even Grandma and Grandpa. Eliminate a laundry list of "don'ts." The first rule is "walking only" when we are indoors. Ask the child about running in the house. You should get a response to the effect that we shouldn't run. Compliment the response and repeat the behavior you prefer: "This is a house where we all walk from one place to another." Continue with two more rules, choosing things that are most important to you and follow the pattern by stating the behavior that you desire.

Ask why these rules are important. You may need to provide some help, maybe not. Of course, we are talking about civility in this situation, and self-control. For reinforcement, ask the child to tell you the rules at the library, for example, or at church. The reasons are the same—consideration of others and sometimes our own safety. Tailor the specifics and your language to the age(s) of your grandchildren.

By using this technique you will be defining and encouraging behaviors that represent *civility* and *character*—even *citizenship*—in a nonjudgmental way. You have circumvented the need to issue advance criticism, and the child knows how people are expected to behave at your house even though you haven't said *don't* once! In subsequent situations, you may ask your grandchild's assistance in stating the good behavior rules for other places you may go together. How about a review before you enter the grocery store? This technique helps support the child's self-confidence by describing what is expected of them in different circumstances.

Does this argument against criticism mean that you and I are never going to feel critical? We all will; it's inevitable. But professionals bring their skills and experience to the job. First, stop and think about how you feel when you are criticized, even now, at your age. Second, recall and remember that learning to do the right thing includes trying and failing, testing the rules, and even forgetfulness. Third, train yourself and practice the idea that you needn't directly criticize much of anything. More often than not it is preferable to accentuate the positive, ask leading questions, and help clarify what you expect the youngster to do. Your chances are much better that the child will attempt to live up to the standard when their own personal consultant can confirm the evidence that shows the young person's capacity to do so.

Actively grab opportunities to confirm a child's better decisions, and don't stand by waiting only to point out deficiencies. We can be influential models for demonstrating an alternative method when criticism seems to be the order of the day. Fourth, just imagine yourself criticizing that important business client who spilled the wine at dinner when you feel the urge to criticize your grandchild.

Does This Advice Apply to Teenagers?

Sometimes we wish that teenaged grandchildren would experiment a little less! The basic premise of criticism as defeating and insulting doesn't change even though the nature of their experimentation can be more ominous. Parents, of course, are on the front line when it comes to teen behavior. Still, the advice of the experts on how to criticize so that teens will listen applies just as readily to grandparents. Don't be quick to attack. Remember to criticize the behavior but not the person. Share your wisdom by offering a preferable alternative.

In a book devoted to dealing with teens, Elkind concedes that there is a place for constructive criticism. However, it should be motivated by our caring and respect. Proceeding with caution is advisable, he suggests, because we will be most effective if we have our own emotions under control.[14] In fact, when teens are acting most childish it is even more incumbent on adults to act like adults. Model the behavior values that you want to see them display and treat your teenaged grandchild like an honored guest or your own best friend. Act as though you want to stay friends.

Why Not Be Blunt About Mistakes Made by Teenagers?

I wouldn't go so far as to suggest that we completely eliminate the direct approach but thinking before we speak is advisable. Many teens are uncertain enough as it is and strong criticism leaves them without a sense of dignity. Confrontational pronouncements may only reinforce some of their own self-doubts. Ask questions first to get the facts straight or to understand the teen's point of view. Remember that children and teenagers evaluate themselves based on the opinions we have of them. When we use harsh words, biting comments, or a sarcastic tone of voice, we defeat our own good intentions.[15]

Remember Your Pledge to Think Like an Entrepreneur?

A part of your preparation in the creation and production of an excellent consultation should be to rehearse. If necessary, try on an attitude adjustment in the areas of praise, rewards, and criticism. Always think in terms of your new role as a consultant. Let go of the image of yourself as a parent who is responsible for discipline. Let go of that attitude of correction. Remember that your own feelings will be revealed in your facial expressions, in your body language, and through the words that you choose to use.

The urge to praise or criticize is immediate and spontaneous. Practice conversations in your mind so that you will have a few handy, all-purpose words or phrases at the ready which are neither critical nor demeaning. See yourself talking respectfully to the grandchildren of your best friend in your friend's presence. Use the same care with your own grandchildren.

SUMMARY

The material in Part Seven was intended to polish our interactive skills for consulting successfully with our grandchildren.

We are now prepared to put the pieces together in Part Eight and to explore the details concerning the delivery of our services.

A JOB DESCRIPTION FOR GRANDPARENTS (Part 6)

Consulting is no fly-by-night operation; we can't afford to engage in *The Business of Life* without a plan, management techniques, or interpersonal skills. The tools of relationship building, when combined with interviewing techniques, are vital. In fact, they are the very substance of the business when it comes to competent grandparenting.

BUSINESS OF LIFE GRANDPARENT (Part 6)
JOB CONTENT

The highest level of excellence in customer service shall be the goal of every consultant.

(To be continued.)

PART EIGHT

THE BIRTHDAY PROGRAM

The idea for *The Birthday Program* evolved from several sources. By sharing the ideas, the memories, and the feelings that went into the crafting of this event, I hope to show you its full potential.

Early on, it became apparent that there were compelling reasons to focus this annual consultation on each grandchild's birthday. At first, it seemed appropriate to make this event as natural a part of life as possible, and that alone seemed to be reason enough. However, other more subtle benefits slowly emerged. I realized that the repetition of a birthday event would result in an annual ritual and that led me to explore the nature and benefits of rituals in our lives.

As the implications and possibilities grew, I knew that you and I could take this new grandparenting job opportunity and turn it into something special just as I sensed that we really could act together—independently—and make a difference.

Here, then, is a brief look at the realm that's hidden from view as you conduct *The Birthday Program*. Thereafter, we move on to the thoroughly practical matters of implementation.

CHAPTER 24. Rituals

The more I thought about the regularity and consistency of the ideas I had in mind for our *Birthday Program* consultations, the more I became intrigued by their ritual nature. Rituals and ceremonies are regular features of life. Many are seemingly ordinary routines of daily living while others are occasional and very distinctive. Routine events give us a sense of certainty and comfort.

Rituals make us feel special and a part of something important. We have family rituals that are ours by the accident of our birth such as family reunions or annual family vacations at the lake. In other cases, we join an organization that has its own patterns of admission and membership, and participation in those rituals confers a sense of belonging.

Tell your grandchild that he or she has been chosen to share a special birthday talk that is just for the two of you. (We will consider the question of sharing *The Birthday Program* with your spouse in another chapter.) It will always be private and no one else will know what you talk about. Say that it is a special privilege just for a grandparent and a grandchild.

You might want to reveal that you plan to keep a record of the topics and someday you will give a finished album to the child that tells the story of these special talks. Use your own words in a similar vein but make it a distinct and privileged event. Repeat this message through as many birthdays as necessary for the child to anticipate your annual tête-à-tête.

Perhaps the question, "What did you discover *this* year?" will become a whispered code message that you will share for years and years. Perhaps you will devise your own secret signal for getting started. This is just the sort of thing that would appeal to kids in the preteen years. There are many opportunities for you to be creative in this venture.

Perhaps you will decide to spend a little time reminiscing about the things you discussed the previous year or looking at a picture that you put in the memory book. This album, *My Book of Birthdays,* is an integral part of *Business of Life* consulting. A unique format has been designed to accompany this *New-Fashioned Grandparenting* book and will be described in Chapter 28. It is intended to be a permanent record and an active reminder of topics and issues that have been discussed. Sharing memories on a regular basis is often part of the process of ritual events.

As you listen, you might share a few comments about the child's mother or father that show how the parent discovered an important lesson about life. (Do this only if it is pertinent to the discussion.) You will be reinforcing family identity and continuity as well as the value or behavior that prompted the story. Rituals often include memories of past times.

Ritual and ceremony are said to lift our spirits and to reinforce our values.[1] Because each of us will be on our own, individual creativity will reign supreme.

I am eager to learn about the variety of ideas that may emerge from this notion of ritual and ceremony. Will you choose to light a small, special candle that will burn during your talk? Will the two of you create your own opening or closing prayer to be repeated at each annual visit? Maybe you and a granddaughter will weave secret friendship bracelets out of yarn and wear them during your special talk. Or will you make up a short pledge to repeat each time before you start? Perhaps the two of you will agree to absolutely always take a birthday walk during your birthday talk no matter what the weather!

Not only am I interested in your experiences as you work with *The Birthday Program,* including the ritual elements, but I believe that all of us will benefit from sharing our discoveries. Please turn to the information included near the end of this book for directions on how to stay in touch.

Are Rituals Really That Important?

The late Joseph Campbell is well known for his work on myths. He interpreted much of what we know and do in light of ancient myths, rituals, and ceremonies. In his writing, he lamented the absence of meaningful rituals in the lives of children and young people in American society today. He was particularly concerned about the loss of symbols and rituals that signify a major transition from one stage of life to another.[2]

From his own life experience, he took the example of short trousers, which visibly separated young boys from the more mature, older youths who were allowed to wear long pants. In so doing, these older boys looked more like men. The day when he could finally graduate to long pants clearly symbolized an important growth step in his life. This is an

THE BIRTHDAY PROGRAM

example of a public marker and a ritual that quite visibly separated the men from the boys.[3]

Take a few moments to remember your own youthful experiences with rituals. In *Rituals For Our Times*, the authors remind us that the evening meal, when family members are gathered together, is a significant ritual even though we don't often think of it in such terms today when it is far less common.[4] Many of us are likely to have had this regular experience and probably took it for granted at the time. Now, we can appreciate its value.

Did you participate in Scouting? When you think about it now, does it seem to you that this popular activity incorporated ritual events?

I remember being a Girl Scout. By reviewing this experience in my own life, I was able to recognize many of the simple elements that constitute a ritual event. Although you may have been a Boy Scout, let me introduce the Girl Scout's Promise as it was then. Picture us with right hands raised, wearing our uniforms and badge sashes. Here is what the girls said,

> *On my honor I will try*
> *To do my duty to God and my country.*
> *To help others at all times.*
> *To obey the Girl Scout Laws.*

Although this pledge has been modified since my time, a quick count reveals six separate values: honor, duty, obedience, God, country, and helping others. This ritual recitation confirmed our membership in an exclusive group with its own special words and clothing which served to reinforce group identity, and it called for the repetition of our group values.

Our commitment was expressed through our activities, many of which were service oriented, but there were also many varied skills that could be acquired. As an adult, I realized that the process that culminated in the receipt of another badge was very instructive. From beginning to end, the ritual process, including the periodic award ceremony, was so simple and so satisfying.

My Scouting experience was a very normal, routine part of my life. I don't know whether or not Scouting was at its height during those war years and the decade after, but I do feel now that it fit in with the kind of performance expectations that were the norm during my youth and probably yours.

I am confident that each of you can find important elements of ritual and ceremony in your youth. They gave us a measure of stability, they organized the flow of time, and provided us with a sense of continuity. They gave us standards, ideals, and values that helped to mold our character and our behavior.

As for other shared national rituals, induction into the armed services once counted as a major transition ritual from boyhood to manhood. Campbell also noted that Mother Nature provides a physical transition for girls moving into womanhood, which in some cultures is still accompanied by recognition rituals.[5]

As a society, the common rituals that now mark the transition to adulthood are the acquisition of a driver's license and high school graduation. Ritual and ceremony, however, are seen only in the graduation event.

When asked about the growing focus in Western culture on the individual, Campbell responded that all people crave ceremony and meaning. We still need the assurance that we are a part of something important that is larger than ourselves. In the absence of cultural rituals for symbolically attaining manhood, for example, he believed that teenage gangs have filled the gap by providing their own initiation ceremonies, their own "uniforms," and setting up their own definitions of adult behavior.[6] It doesn't take gang membership to see that teens dress in clothing and accessories that are selected for identification with their group and the sense of belonging that that brings.

Think about *The Business of Life Annual Meeting* in the light of this emphasis on ritual and ceremony, remembering their absence in much of modern life. Ask yourself if *The Birthday Program* exemplifies this description: "Rituals provide familiar anchor points and protected time and space to stop and reflect on life's transformations."[7] Protected time and space . . . a small treasure that can be provided by an annual grandparenting ritual.

CHAPTER 25. Origins of *The Birthday Program*

Because I began by using a business analogy in order to support our stature as professionals, the standard, corporate annual meeting became the first possibility that I entertained for a grandparent/grandchild conversation.

The conclusion of a corporation's business year is marked by this distinctive event. Held wherever the corporate headquarters are located and attended by the officers, board members, and stockholders of the company, this meeting includes an informative report on the status of the business and its prospects for the coming year. A great deal of the information provided concerns financial matters. These data and their analysis show comparisons with past performance and may define numerical goals for the new year. The associated document, the annual report, summarizes this material and must, by law, divulge certain financial and technical information. Of course, annual reports are also used as marketing tools, which means that they now contain multicolored pictures and graphics as well.

The annual meeting itself provides an opportunity for shareholders to question company leaders. Refreshments may be provided. It is often a celebration, especially if things have gone well in the previous year and good news is on the horizon.

Because corporate fiscal years do not necessarily coincide with the start of the calendar year, annual meetings are held throughout the year all over the country.

Already, you can see some of the elements in the business world that support our mission in the grandparenting business.

Your *Business of Life Annual Meeting* is an event that has been designed to take place every year, year after year. This repetition will give you the opportunity to put all of your knowledge and skills into play while conducting a review and analysis of the events and lessons that your grandchild experienced during the previous year. Obviously your grandchild's participation is required. How, I wondered, would we choose a date that would work for everyone?

Origins of *The Birthday Program*

Of course, there is really only one answer that makes any sense for grandparents. The date that represents an end and a beginning, much like the corporate meeting, would be the birthday of each and every grandchild.

When we think about events that already occur regularly in our lives, birthdays stand out. Birthdays are clearly ritualized in our culture. A birthday is a dependable feature of life. It appears with absolute regularity every year for every one of us. This special day that belongs to each of us, returns again and again whether we are looking forward to its arrival or making every effort to avoid it.

What none of us can avoid is the meaning of this day, the certainty that our life is evolving or moving through time, and that we are inevitably changing. Our birthdays literally count the years. The numbers alone seem to make us grow older.

Birthdays are the markers or transition points for a new time period that will bring us new events, new problems to solve, and new opportunities.

Birthdays sometimes let us slough off an old persona, as when we finally become a teenager or when we reach that magic number that means we can acquire a driver's license.

For the Baby Boomers, the 30th year was once an acknowledged definition of old age, whereas it is now becoming more and more common for 100th birthdays to be celebrated. For a child, a birthday is a time of presents and parties, a transition from the age I was yesterday to the new number that can be claimed today. Clearly, at any age it is a mark of distinction and a special event.

It is apparent that a birthday, because of its regularity and its meaning, is a natural opportunity for the inauguration of a new grandparent/grandchild tradition.

If a normal birthday can be adapted for *The Business of Life Annual Meeting*, there is another recognizable event that serves to illustrate the content of such a meeting, and that event is New Year's Eve. New Year's Eve arrives as dependably as one's birthday.

New Year's Eve puts adults on the brink of possibility, the possibility of change. It is another kind of milestone, another transition which many adults acknowledge by voluntarily, but secretly, making a resolution.

THE BIRTHDAY PROGRAM

Traditionally, each of us makes our own personal commitment to improvements that we plan to make in our lives in the coming year. This comes about because we review our past behavior and set new goals. We pledge, we vow, we promise to do better. We give ourselves a year's time or perhaps a lesser, yet specific, time period in which to correct some deficiency in our behavior or our habits. We resolve to give up smoking or to lose weight, for example. We expect to monitor our performance and we set performance standards for ourselves.

The traditional New Year's resolution combines a personal evaluation of the year just completed and a commitment to making improvements in the coming year.

These features played a subtle role, which can be appreciated by adults, in the formation of *The Birthday Program* concept. Although we won't want to engage in a rigid or rote exercise that mimics New Year's Eve, the general pattern of reviewing the past and anticipating the future, with goals in mind, is a skill that children can gradually develop. If we overlay this philosophy on the annual meeting, together they reinforce the purpose of *The Birthday Program* consultation.

When I refer to an annual meeting for business purposes and the New Year's resolution, I do so only to fix known references in our own adult minds. They are examples which allow us to share a common understanding of the purpose and content of *The Birthday Program*. They are irrelevant and unimportant to children or teenagers, whereas they have very real meaning for grandparents.

Here, then, is the basic formula for the primary *Business of Life* event:

A corporate annual meeting
plus
A birthday
plus
New Year's Eve
equals
The Business of Life concept for
New-fashioned Grandparenting
called
The Birthday Program.

How Could We Design a New Tradition?

We bring together management (grandparents) and shareholders (grandchildren). We transform the speeches and audience questions of a corporate meeting into a creative consultation. We adapt the annual meeting's traditional oral reports by conducting a review and discussion of a grandchild's learning experiences in the past year. We adapt the written reports, having maintained our records, and then we document the highlights of each birthday consultation in our own version of an annual report. You will find that Chapter 28 explains the content of the special album titled, *My Book of Birthdays*.

We note the grandchild's birthday as a growth marker and we incorporate the New Year's Eve tradition of performance evaluation and goal setting into the discussion.

These simple features form the framework for your *Business of Life* franchise.

How Practical and Realistic Is This Idea?

First of all, I expect that you will be in attendance at birthday time, if it is at all possible. That's a point in favor of *The Birthday Program*. There is no need to create another event when we can make use of one at hand. It is unlikely that any of us will forget the date. The experience is completely personal within your own family, but this gives us a whole new way to make those birthdays meaningful. Each year the process is the same, but the content changes right along with the growth of your grandchild.

Although we adults have a broad, multiyear perspective on the entire process, from our grandchildren's point of view the annual meeting will simply be thought of as the time for a special talk with Grampa or Nana on her or his birthday.

I believe that the addition of this regular, private conversation with each of your grandchildren, one that recurs every year on each grandchild's birthday, can become a cherished event that evolves into a ritual. And I firmly believe in the importance and the staying power of rituals.

On the surface we are dealing with a simple idea. It is in the execution of the idea that skill and sophistication will be in evidence. Exceptional execution will yield exceptional results and repetition will secure the impact.

CHAPTER 26. Getting Started

Now that you understand the origins of new-fashioned grandparenting, we can review the components of *The Birthday Program* event itself.

Each annual meeting becomes a special time for the two of you, you and the birthday grandchild, to talk about some of the child's activities during the past year and to think about the coming year.

All of your preparation comes to fruition in this birthday conversation. You have done your research so that you have some knowledge of your grandchild's world. You have contemplated age-appropriate topics. You have practiced creating opening questions. You have reviewed and given considerable thought to the topic of values that represent *The Three C's*: *character*, *civility*, and *citizenship*. You have decided to be creative, to have some fun, and to make an impact, however small it may seem at the time. Those of us who can begin at the beginning with very young children should know that we can relax a bit, because they will be very forgiving as we practice.

The entire focus of *The Business of Life* is a deceptively simple concept: WHAT DID YOU DISCOVER THIS YEAR? Now, I must confess that it is my natural tendency to use the word "learn" instead of "discover." The experts who know about kids and whose material I have reviewed counsel against the actual use of the word "learn." They warn (some go so far as to guarantee) that it will turn off children's attention because it has a thoroughly negative connotation. It sounds a bit too much like schoolwork. Let's accept that advice and use the word "discover" instead. WHAT DID YOU DISCOVER THIS YEAR? It does sound more exciting, doesn't it? Behind the scenes, you and I will know we are interested in their learning experiences, and that is what we really plan to probe and discuss.

Now that we have reviewed child development and possess some pretty good consulting skills, it should be obvious that nothing thus far has given any hint that we intend to preach, punish, or condemn. Neither are we going to use "right" answers in trade for birthday presents.

> **Reminder!**
>
> We will be looking for everyday behaviors that represent good values. *The Birthday Program* is NOT fundamentally about praising the honors won, the trophies received, or the A's awarded. It is NOT intended to be an opportunity for criticism.

The Consultation

Let's look more closely at just what might happen in a *Business of Life* consultation. We find a quiet place and a suitable time. Perhaps we walk together side by side or we sit in a quiet room. We select comfortable seating positions that convey equality rather than dominance. We make lots of eye contact and appear interested and curious—because we are! Our body language is open, casual, and welcoming.

As the managing consultant, you take the lead and guide the conversation. The focus is always on the child. The event should be companionable and productive. You strive to generate a review of the child's experiences by asking lots of open-ended questions. You incorporate a values-based interpretation whenever possible or you ask your grandchild's opinion. You challenge yourself to cover at least one value from each of *The Three C* categories, and you are prepared with samples from the child's experiences.

You listen proactively so that you can respond in a meaningful way. You compliment the good things you hear, endorse good value-based behaviors, remark upon a learning process whenever you detect that one is involved, and offer your thoughts or ask leading questions where there are still problems. Except for the earliest age group when kids want definite answers, you try not to rush to judgment or to supply ready answers as you ask good questions to help the child in making her or his own discovery of solutions. You do not, however, shy away from clarifying what is right or wrong, if necessary. When a strong standard is required, you supply it.

You ask your grandchild to practice specific behaviors in the coming year and you talk about their importance. You give some example and get a commitment. Most children will be interested to know that you make resolutions about things you intend to improve in the coming year. This shows that everyone keeps learning and keeps trying to do things better.

Is It Really That Easy?

What do you suppose some of the inevitable problems and challenges will be? What kinds of surprises are you likely to face at one time or another? When should you adapt and when should you hold firm? And what should be considered as the absolute minimum requirements for this meeting?

First, it isn't really necessary for *The Business of Life Annual Meeting* to take place on the actual birthday. Because of the distance that often exists between grandparents and their grandchildren, it may be necessary to adapt to the circumstances. I have found it necessary to do so. As a result, some of my meetings have occurred quite some time after the actual birthday. Fortunately, really young kids don't know the difference. On the other hand, don't neglect a meeting just because it isn't convenient! Do it by phone if there's no other way. The child should become familiar and comfortable with the routine. We want them to view the meeting as a normal part of life. Once you have begun to establish this ritual and find it necessary to revise your schedule, I would suggest that you say something about the fact that "Your birthday talk got lost somehow, so let's just do it now."

The date, then, is not an absolute thing although we do want to associate our meeting with the fact that the child is a whole year older and that means something! You might say, "The last time we had a birthday talk you had grown and learned so much! Now tell me, what did you discover *this* year?"

Sometimes, despite my preference for a secluded talk, I have had to create an annual conversation in the midst of other family activities. This has happened when a grandchild asked a question or showed me something (homework or a favorite toy) that gave me an opportune lead-in to ask value-based questions. I have occasionally taken those opportunities based on my quick judgment of the likelihood of having a better chance later. I believe this is quite satisfactory for young children although I prefer to interpret these talks as practice sessions. I hope you will eagerly take these chance openings to practice your craft. As a rule, however, I much prefer a separate and private place in order to develop a pattern of open and willing conversation that won't be interrupted.

Second, I want to reemphasize my belief in the fundamental importance of confidentiality when it comes to *Business of Life* grandparenting. In my view, this is a requirement, and I hope you won't feel tempted to disagree unless the situation is truly extreme. That, of course, is a judgment call on your part, and you must make your own decision. If you have established a level of confidence and feel that you must break it, especially with a teenager, don't act in haste. Give yourself a chance to carefully review your decision and its ramifications. Always tell the youngster ahead of time about your concern and the dilemma you are facing over breaking your commitment to confidentiality. (And, by the way, don't assume that the youngster knows the meaning of the word confidential.)

Third, since privacy and confidentiality have been stressed, how should we deal with curious inquiries from other family members? Simply handle them with good humor and suitably general assurances. Tell them whatever you like so long as you do not divulge any depth of content that should remain in confidence. Let them know that you love being a grandparent and that you are enjoying a few quiet moments to get to know your grandchild better.

CHAPTER 27. On-the-Job Training

Now that we share an understanding of the origins, direction, and importance of *Business of Life* consulting, the following practice sessions will outline just a few of the major topics and issues that you will want to consider for your own annual meetings.

BE PREPARED. Start right now. Anticipate, prepare, and practice. Initiate your market research effort. Stay tuned to the current culture. Develop a good awareness of the kinds of problems that kids face today. Some of them have been mentioned in this book; many have not. Be skeptical of dramatic media headlines; investigate. Don't just stick your head in the sand and ignore reality. Remember that you and I are dealing with specific children, not statistics. Know what you are up against in a very real sense but plan to accentuate the positive.

Start as soon as possible to keep and file notes on your grandchild's activities and be sure to jot down the date as you go. Organize the information in a time frame based on the child's birthday so that you can refer to the past year's material easily.

DON'T HESITATE. Start practicing your interviewing techniques. Jump in and get a feel for your talents. Practice on friends and family members both young and old. Learn from this experience and try variations. Use expressions of empathy. Ask open-ended or probing questions to keep a conversation going. Temper your impulse to talk extensively about yourself. Realize that you will have to let some opportunities go. Evaluate yourself. Practice until you feel natural and comfortable in your role.

REMEMBER THIS: The better you become, the better your annual meetings will be. Contrary to popular thinking, you will discover that young children have remarkably long attention spans when a skillful grandparent involves them in conversation and there are no interruptions or distractions.

Why Are We Doing This?

Be prepared for a grandchild's question about why you are doing this over and over. Anticipate it and develop an answer ahead of time. You

On-the-Job Training

may want to create a ritual opening or closing for each birthday conversation that explicitly states the purpose.

Preteens and teenagers alike may need to be reminded that confidentiality is part of the deal. Explain your commitment more than once. Tell them that it is a unique privilege of grandparents who are not required by anyone to divulge personal information. In your own way, let them know that you can be a haven of security and a supportive confidant. Use this topic to introduce gossiping and its effect on people. You might want to explore values that support confidentiality and privacy. This would give you an opportunity to explain the kind of extreme circumstance which would lead you to re-evaluate your commitment. All of this is relevant to teens as they practice forming friendships.

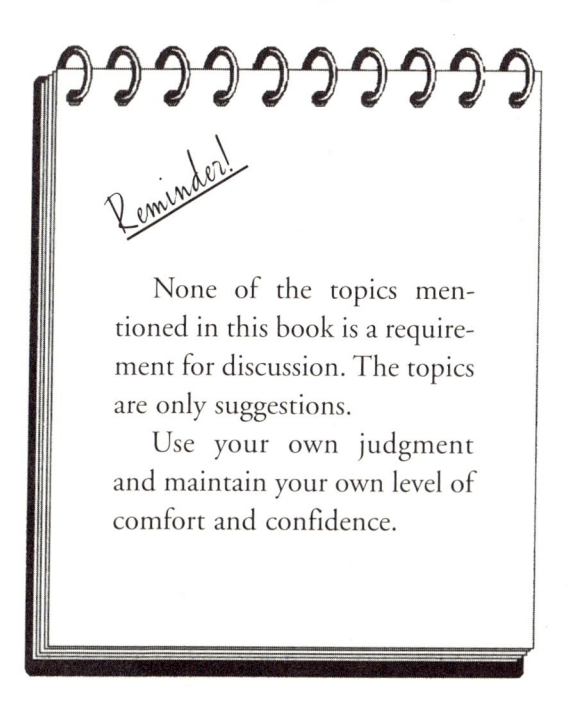

Reminder!

None of the topics mentioned in this book is a requirement for discussion. The topics are only suggestions.

Use your own judgment and maintain your own level of comfort and confidence.

The following pages show topics that you may want to consider, but *don't let them limit your thinking*. Remember the entrepreneurial characteristics that have brought you this far and make these consultations uniquely your own.

THE BIRTHDAY PROGRAM

Children in the 4-7 Age Group

As you review some of the key elements of life for the very youngest group, make an effort to connect some of *The Three C* values with each question.

Remember that this group tends to want answers instead of help thinking things through. You have an opportune time to practice your craft with this age group because they will not have preconceived expectations. *The Birthday Program* will be new to them so you can relax and practice on the job.

As you read these suggestions, practice by thinking of a value and selecting a *Three C* category for each question. Create your own follow-up questions. Make up new ones.

Prepare several responses for those times when a child says, "I don't know."

Home and Family

- Tell me about the difference between boys and girls?
- What does sharing mean? What things do you share at home?
- What do you do to help take care of your baby sister/brother?
- Where do you put your toys at the end of the day?
- How do you help take care of your kitten/dog?
- What is your favorite storybook? Why?

School and Friends

Daycare or nursery school brings exposure to all of the interactive skills that come under *civility* as well as the need for self-control. School also brings new expectations and new responsibilities.

- Do you take turns at nursery school? Why?
- What do you like most about school?
- How should we treat our friends?
- Do you know how to take turns? Why do we do that?
- What do teachers do?
- What do you want to be when you grow up? Why? What do they do?
- Who is your best friend? What do you like most about her/him?
- Which do you like best, reading or arithmetic? Why?

On-the-Job Training

- How does your teacher like to have kids act at school? What difference does it make?
- Your parents told me that you were given a citizenship award at school. What does that mean? What did you do?

<u>Fantasy and Heroes</u>

- Who is you favorite superhero? What do you like about him/her? Do heroes do good things to help people? Do you know any real people who are heroes? What does being a hero mean?
- What do you like to imagine?
- Do you ever make up stories?

<u>New Skills</u>

- Can you ride a two-wheel bike yet? Was it hard to learn how? How does it feel to be able to ride away? Do you always wear your safety helmet?
- Do you like to play any sports? Are you on a team?
- Are you taking piano lessons? Tell me about them.
- What do you play outdoors? Do the kids around here play together just for fun?

<u>Problems and Fears</u>

- At first it can seem scary to go to a big school. How did you feel when you started kindergarten?
- Sometimes there are bullies at school. Do you know of any? Do they make you worry sometimes? How do you handle them?
- Once in a while, I have a bad dream. Does that ever happen to you? What do you do?
- Sometimes grown-up people get mad and yell at each other. I might feel scared if it happened to me. How about you? Do mad people get happy again after a while?

<u>Neighborhood</u>

- Do you know what litter bugs are? What do they do? What is litter? Are you a litter bug? What do firemen do?
- How should we behave when we go to the library? Why?

THE BIRTHDAY PROGRAM

Youth in the 8-11 Age Group

Hint: these kids will relate to the aphorisms that follow this age-related material.

Develop some potential answers to the "Why are we doing this?" question. Take the initiative—ask your grandchild why he or she thinks this conversation is happening.

Express your great curiosity about his life this past year.

Substitute your specific information where I have used general topics in the following questions. Grandmother, for example, didn't ask about sports participation. She asked Dylan about his first experience with golf lessons.

Home and Family

- What chores do you have at home? Why is it important to do your share?
- Your dog sure has grown. What do you do to help take care of him?
- Do you get an allowance? What do you do with it?
- What do you think you want to be when you grow up? Why?
- Who's your favorite hero right now? How does he/she act and why?
- Do you get around on your bike now? Remember how hard it was to learn to ride at first? (Aphorism example: "If at first you don't succeed, try, try again.") How does it make you feel?

School and Friends

- What do you like about school these days? What's your favorite subject? Why?
- What's been really hard to learn in school? Do you have homework? Have you learned how to organize your assignments?
- Do you do your homework on the computer? What are the rules about copying things off the Internet? What is cheating all about?
- What activities do you enjoy with your friends?
- What do you like to do when you are alone? Do you ever daydream?

- Are you involved in any sports activities? What are they? Do you like playing on a team? What does sportsmanship mean? Who is your favorite sports hero? Why do you admire him/her? What qualities does a hero have?

Neighborhood and Community
- Tell me about your neighbors. Do you have a friend your age on this street?
- Have you tried mowing lawns for extra money?
- What do you do to help that nice, old couple down the street?
- Who is supposed to keep things clean in this neighborhood?
- Who owns the park in your neighborhood? Who takes care of it?
- What does you family do to help other people?
- What is graffiti? How do you feel about it?

Problems and Fears
- What do you worry about?
- What kinds of problems do you kids have these days?
- Are there any real mean kids around here? How do you handle them?

Your Future
- What are you looking forward to?

Early Adolescents in the 12-15 Age Group

Once again, express interest in your grandchild's life and activities of the past year. You might comment on how strange and mixed up life gets at about this age.

Remember that kids like to imagine themselves a year or two older and more mature than they really are. Give them the benefit of the doubt. Remind yourself to be calm and relaxed. Be optimistic about the future but don't brush off a teen's concerns lightly.

This age period can be the point when you review and update your techniques. Polish your conversation skills. Understand that the questions you ask a teenager help that youngster identify the topics that you feel comfortable with. Sometimes it can be helpful to bring up a subject indirectly. For example, you could say, "I read about _____." (which makes it impersonal) or "I was surprised to learn that many teens feel _____. What do you and your friends think about it?" Referring to an unnamed/unknown person lets a teen attribute his or her uncertainty or embarrassment to anonymous others.

Here are a few questions that will help when you want to accentuate the positive. They are supplied by specialists who provide advice on how to support a youngster's self-image. They can be effective all during teen years and may be useful in supporting adult children as they grapple with the many demands of family and work.

Use your conversations skills to probe for more depth and detail following these leading questions.

- Tell me something you really like about yourself.
- Tell me something that you felt good about this year.
- Tell me something that you think you did well.
- Tell me about something that you really enjoyed this past year.[1]

As often as possible, compliment good values that your grandchild expresses and help explore their meaning in more depth. Recognize conflicting values and help in the process of making value judgments. Inquire about the behavior of friends and comment on the values that they are testing. Don't be afraid to talk directly about what is right and what is wrong—just don't lecture.

<u>Home and Family</u>

- How is life at home these days?
- What do your folks think about the clothes you're wearing? (Note: consider teen clothing as theatrical costuming. They try on various personalities externally as well as internally. Don't criticize in a mean-spirited way, but share your impressions. Try to balance unfavorable comments with something positive.)
- Everyone in my family seemed to be a stranger when I was your age. Do you ever feel that way?
- You've gotten really tall since I saw you last. Does it feel strange?

On-the-Job Training

- What do you watch on TV these days? Why those shows?
- What do you use your computer for? Do you like the chat rooms?

School and Friends

- Are you and _____ still best friends? Why or why not? Do you get together with a group of friends to have fun? Are there kids at school that you don't want to be friends with? Why not? How do they act? (Admit that everyone likes to have friends, but speculate on peer pressure when it comes to making decisions about what to wear and how to behave. Sometimes it's important to think things through for yourself.)
- What have you been studying this year? Is there a subject that you really love? Tell me about your favorite teacher. What do you like best about the way she/he works with students?
- Have you joined any school clubs this last year?
- What kind of music do you like?
- Hey, it was great to hear that you're on the (baseball, soccer, gymnastics) team. How's it going?
- Is your homework getting harder? Is it tempting to cheat sometimes? What happens when we cheat? How does it feel? What do we learn? Do we cheat ourselves in any way? Does it make a person feel proud? What about someone who cheats once in a while versus never or all of the time?
- What are you doing after school before Mom and Dad get home?

Neighborhood and Community

- What do you know about ecology?
- What would it take to make the world a better place?
- Do kids your age get involved in community service projects these days?
- How do you feel about all the graffiti on those buildings in town?
- Do you think that recycling makes any difference? Is it worth the time and effort?

THE BIRTHDAY PROGRAM

- Have you ever heard of Arbor Day? Why should we plant more trees, anyway?
- What are elections about? What does a city mayor do? How does someone become president of this country? Have you considered running for a class office at school?
- Your birthday is pretty close to the Fourth of July. What do we celebrate on that day? (Use other holidays, as appropriate.)

<u>Problems and Concerns</u>

- What was the most troubling thing you discovered last year?
- Tell me about the hardest thing you had to figure out this year.
- What was your most difficult challenge this year? How did you resolve it? What steps did you take? Did you feel discouraged? Are you still working on it?
- How does it feel after you have learned something that was difficult in the beginning?
- I suppose you know kids who are experimenting with _____. How do you feel about it?
- What is the worst problem the world faces?

The topic of developing sexuality is a primary feature of this age and stage. Your involvement will be circumscribed by whether or not you are the same sex as your grandchild. If you are the same gender, you share a common experience. Being the opposite sex can be very helpful because you have a different experience and point of view.

Everything about this subject is probably relevant to your grandchild, even if he or she acts nonchalant. The topic of sexuality can refer to the changes occurring in the child's body as well as to interest in the opposite sex. Don't be pushy about specifics, but try to create openings by asking good questions. And please, don't force yourself to go beyond your own level of comfort with this topic because your feelings will probably show. You could, however, find age-appropriate books for teens and send them to your grandchild.

Here are a few possibilities to get you started.

- Do you have a group of friends, both boys and girls, who do things together? Are you and your friends starting to date?

On-the-Job Training

- Do you ever watch soap operas? What do you think about the way people behave on those shows? They sure focus on sex a lot. Can you talk with Mom or Dad about what you see? (It may be smart to find out how involved the parents are in talking about sexuality.)
- Does your school have a course on families and relationships? Is it embarrassing to ask questions in class? I remember feeling that way, and I really wanted to know about _____.

The following exercise, IMAGINE: Exercise Number Six, is intended to help you remember your youth and to let you experiment in order to find "your own voice."

> **IMAGINE:
> Exercise
> Number Six**

The Actor

Pretend that you are playing a part on stage in a small, intimate theater. You have been cast as a wise adult and you will be talking to a young teenager about life and relationships. Set the scene and improvise. Create your own monologue and practice your lines.

Notice that the teen is feigning casual attention. You might talk about how hard it was for you to find information and good advice when you were young. Admit that you felt bewildered and confused. Search your memories and think about what bothered you most.

What was the big secret about sex? What kind of information would have helped you most? What is the most important thing to understand?

THE BIRTHDAY PROGRAM

WORKSHEET For IMAGINE: Exercise Number Six

This exercise should stimulate a stream of recollections about your own transition from pre-teen to adolescent. It wasn't entirely sex and hormones and relationships. Brain development prompted those questions about the meaning of life and other philosophical issues.

First, make a short list of the topics and worries and dreams and frustrations that you once felt and thought about. Be honest with yourself.

_____

_____

_____

_____

_____

_____

_____

_____

_____

_____

_____

Second, compose a succinct monologue for a specific grandchild whom you are hoping to guide through this period of life. Its purpose is to indicate that you are open to listening and advising during this time because you once had this experience. You may want to endorse talking with Mom or Dad and position yourself as a backup. If you and this grandchild aren't the same gender, you may want to indicate that you can be helpful in explaining things about the opposite sex. Work on this until you feel you can make a smooth but candid delivery.

Adolescents in the 16-19 Age Group

For older teens in this age group, many values have been consolidated, but others still haven't been tested. Those challenges and experiences are still ahead of them. You really are talking with someone who is approaching adulthood but don't slip into superficial chats. The transition from high school to college or to adult employment is a very important time.

<u>Home and Family</u>
- How do you feel about the rules and expectations your parents have for you as you get older?
- What kind of an example do you feel that you set for your younger siblings?
- Do you feel as though you have grown up (matured) in this last year? In what ways?

<u>School and Friends</u>
- Have you found that you like different kinds of people as you get older? Why?
- Which adults do you admire?
- Do you have a student government at school? Are you participating?

THE BIRTHDAY PROGRAM

- Have you joined any of the school clubs this year?
- What do you plan to do when you graduate from high school?
- Tell me about your college preparations. What options are you looking at?

<u>Neighborhood and Community</u>
- Is driver's training required where you live?
- Where do you stand on the drinking and driving issue? How do your friends feel about this subject?
- What kind of volunteer projects are you working on?

<u>Employment and Finances</u>
- What is the definition of a *good employee?*
- What kind of work attitudes do you find among your co-workers? Do they respect the products and property of the owner? How do you feel about that?
- Has your job experience influenced your own career goals?
- How does our use of money show our values? Do you have your own budget?
- How do you plan to help pay for college?
- What is the best kind of investment for someone in your position?

<u>Questions and Concerns</u>
- There are some tough problems in the world right now. Do you think the average person can do anything about them?
- What is your opinion about discrimination? What is the worst kind? What should we be doing about it?
- How do you react to disappointment? What if you don't get a grade that you feel you deserved?
- When have you felt afraid? How do you deal with fear? What is the meaning of courage?
- What challenged you most this past year? Did you become discouraged? Are you still working on it?
- What are your best talents and skills? Can you make a career of them?
- What was your most satisfying accomplishment this year?

Your Future

- Do you dream about your future? How will you make your dreams come true?
- Tell me about what you might like to do with your life.
- Do you sense that you have a purpose in life?
- What kinds of options are you evaluating?
- What's on your mind these days?
- What are you looking forward to in the next year?

A Supplementary Activity for Talking with Teens

Letter writing seems so old-fashioned, but it remains a wonderful way to communicate and it can be just the right choice when it comes to touchy issues and teenagers. You can instruct indirectly by referring to unnamed "others" or articles you have read or memories that you have as a way to bring up important issues that may be too embarrassing to talk about face-to-face.

Relationships and sexual matters are obvious topics that can be discussed in writing. Good information can be supplied while embarrassment is reduced. You may not want to wait until a distant birthday. If you are comfortable enough to be able to deal with sexual topics calmly and objectively and if you can write a letter without an accusing or demanding tone, you may find this an excellent means of introducing important information that can be received in private.

Perhaps an article that you have just read will become a springboard for your comments. You might express curiosity about what teens today think about a subject—premarital sex, for example, or AIDS. If you adopt a nonintrusive and nonthreatening style and yet remain accurate about the information you include, you can explain and share a great deal.

You might choose to reminisce about what it was like to be a teenager at a time when there was very little information available about sex or anyone to really talk to about it. Briefly describe how that felt. Express your empathy for youngsters of today who may have the same problem. Conversely, you could point out that there seems to be lots of information now but speculate on its real value. Author Blume reminds us that "kids can sense their parents' fear and discomfort, so they go elsewhere for their information."[2]

A letter gives you a chance to discuss emotions and feelings, doubts, and fears that you and your grandchild might be uncomfortable with in a face-to-face discussion.

If you decide to pursue this method, there is a range of topics that matter in a teenager's life that you might want to explore. Tread lightly and with respect. Don't succumb to preaching, but do include your beliefs and standards.

Don't wait until you are asked for information to begin writing letters. Generate them on your own and write on any topic.

Prepare a draft and then be your own best critic. Edit and rewrite. Ask someone else, your spouse or a good friend, for comments. Wait a day or two before mailing your final copy. Don't anticipate receiving correspondence in return. Don't even expect that your efforts will be acknowledged, especially if sex is the topic. Can you understand why they might not be? Think carefully before you interpret your grandchild's silence as rejection of your effort or of the information. Kids will certainly react differently to this offering. They may be enormously glad of the information, yet never mention it directly.

Of course, sex isn't the only topic that lends itself to writing. If you enjoy this kind of communication and learn to do it well, there is a better than even chance that your efforts will pay off most of the time. And don't hesitate to make it clear that you would enjoy a response! Ask for the teenager's thoughts on the material that you write about or raise specific questions.

I am constantly surprised to hear about this or that person who just loves to receive mail. In a time of telephones and E-mail, this old-fashioned method of sharing and caring still seems to delight many of us. I would like to think that most youngsters would be more than happy to receive mail of their very own. It's still a tangible message that says the recipient is special.

As for timely material, our print and electronic media provide an endless stream of issues. The events of your own daily life can be transformed into discussion topics if the message is universal. Remember my own story about the man at the grocery store. The choices you make, the level of detail you present, and the words you choose should all be based on your knowledge of the youngster, including her or his level of mental and moral development.

Even letter writing can become part of this grand adventure. A grandchild's response can be saved in her or his file (the one you are keeping) so that it will become a part of the documentation that you add to the keepsake, *My Book of Birthdays* (Chapter 28).

How About Using an Aphorism Now and Then?

Remember those simple little sayings that seemed to encapsulate a basic truth, give advice on how to behave, or show correct decision making—sayings that seemed to be available on any given topic? Let's not deprive our grandchildren any longer. They still work as handy reminders for many good values. In fact, the first one in the following list was new to my ears when it was recited to me by one of my grandsons.

I include a *Three C* category with each saying, but you can be even more specific by naming the actual value or the self-control behavior that is implied. These sayings are good memory guides for kids to know and remember.

- Gimme, gimme never gets. Please and thank you are best bets. (Civility)
- If at first you don't succeed, try, try again. (Character)
- Practice makes perfect. (Character)
- Think before you speak. (Civility)
- Say what you mean and mean what you say. (Character)
- Anything worth doing is worth doing well. (Character)
- Waste not, want not. (Character)
- Cleanliness is next to godliness. (Character)
- Opportunity may only knock once. (Character)
- A place for everything and everything in its place. (Character)
- There's no time like the present. (Character)
- Never put off till tomorrow what you can do today. (Character)
- It isn't whether you win or lose, but how you play the game. (Character)

- Paddle your own canoe. (Character)
- Do it right the first time. (Character)
- Finish what you start. (Character)
- Honesty is the best policy. (Character)
- Happiness is a difficult job well done. (Character, Civility, Citizenship)
- He or she is just a fair weather friend. (lack of Character and Civility)
- An ounce of prevention is worth a pound of cure. (Character)
- Always let your conscience be your guide. (Character)
- Where there's a will, there's a way. (Character)
- Mind over matter. (Character)
- It's not what you think about, but what you do and say that count. (Civility and Citizenship)

You may also recognize these newer sayings.

- Wherever you go, there you are.
- Plan your work, then work your plan.
- What goes around comes around.

Don't hesitate to make additions if your personal favorite has been overlooked. Correlate a few of these aphorisms with the discussion topics that you prepare in advance of the birthday meeting.

CHAPTER 28. *My Book of Birthdays*

Slip back in time and remember, for a moment, the arrival of your own first child. Did you receive or purchase a baby book for recording all the particulars of those incredible first experiences? Did you paste in the hospital picture and note all the essential details for posterity? How many pages did you fill in? How old was the baby when you tapered off? Did you have a second or third child? How many pages were filled in their baby books? Ah, well . . . those years were so busy!

Now we have the chance to redeem ourselves at a time when we are likely to have a little more time and some perspective, as well. So why not

My Book of Birthdays

give yourself another chance? It's never too late. With *The Business of Life* as the umbrella concept, you will find it easy and enjoyable to prepare a special keepsake album for your grandchild that commemorates the series of *Birthday Program* consultations that the two of you have shared. And, like the baby book, this is a continuous activity.

Let's revisit the baby book idea by changing it to suit *The Birthday Program*. By choosing to follow *The Business of Life* process, you will gain the opportunity to complete a special book for a special child. This version is called *My Book of Birthdays,* and it represents a new opportunity to leave a written record of meaningful lessons in the life of your grandchild. In keeping with the orientation of new-fashioned grandparenting, this record emphasizes the experiences of growth and learning.

This time, keeping a record of your birthday conversations becomes a joy. It is, in effect, an annual report in a very condensed format. *My Book of Birthdays* summarizes the topics that were discussed at each of your annual meetings. It also gives you and your grandchild the chance to review the contents of last year's meeting. There is actually a dual benefit to be derived from recording and keeping this material. You might choose to begin each new session with a brief review of last year's topics. That would help to reinforce the ritual. It is also likely to delight most kids and it will help them realize that they have indeed changed and grown since last year.

A loose-leaf binder will give you the option of adding pages at will. The current craze for creating artistic photo albums could provide inspiration for your work. Or, if you're a straightforward Granddad, a clean and simple style might be just right.

I recommend that you do a minimum summary page which can stand alone if you prefer to be concise. For maximum efficiency, use a template that can simply be filled in each year. Do have several blank sheets prepared ahead of time so that you won't be tempted to put off recording the highlights until later. By then you may not have a good, rich memory of the event.*

---

*Design your own or use the album created to complement this book. (See the back pages of this book for information on how to order.)

THE BIRTHDAY PROGRAM

I have experimented with taking notes during the conversation because the content can range among many topics. Sometimes I remember important points after the conversation and find them valuable. Previously, in the chapter on record keeping, I suggested that you might also consider using a tape recorder. If you do, you won't miss a thing.

You will want to have a place to record the date, location, and the birthday number. The content of the discussion will be more fluid and you may report this material as you wish. The point, however, is to note values, good behaviors, and discoveries or lessons learned. If you decide upon an opening or closing ritual, be sure to include a description and record the words you say. Add fun things now and then, things you laughed over or choice words from the youngster, so that the information is lively and has kid appeal, as well.

You and your grandchild may want to make this record a joint project. Offer to include something special that he or she has created: a drawing, a written memory, a dream, or perhaps a goal for the coming year.

One of the best ways to make this personal is to add a picture, and do make that a picture of both of you, together. This photo can be taken at any time during your birthday visit. It should not intrude upon your private time.

Keep the album in your possession, but share it during your yearly meeting if you care to. Let your grandchild be the guide. Some kids will take delight in this history, others will be, or will profess to be, indifferent. It will be something that you can appreciate should you want to review it and reminisce. Of course, the idea is that you will ultimately transfer ownership to your grandchild.

SUMMARY

In Part Eight, we explored the origins of *The Birthday Program* and considered its potential as a new ritual for childhood and teen years. Next, we turned to the practical circumstances of consulting by reviewing sample questions and topics for each age group. Advance preparation is essential, although in real life you will be training yourself while on the job. Along the way you will be keeping notes and planning future conversations so that you will be prepared to record each year's highlights in the special album called *My Book of Birthdays*. These chapters, taken together, encompass the implementation of your franchise in *The Business of Life*.

It is truly impossible to put into words what you will experience in a *Business of Life* conversation with your own grandchild. You and I can learn and practice. We can be prepared and practical and yet our grandchildren will still manage to amaze and delight us and sometimes to shock and worry us, too. Keep your equilibrium. Fake it if you have to once in a while.

Remember that our hope is to impart some bits of wisdom that will be retained. If we only succeed in showing them how deeply important the art of listening really is, perhaps we will have done enough. It is difficult to know how high to aim. It is important to keep trying and learning.

In Part Nine, we will review our role, take in some issues that are part of the real world experience of new-fashioned grandparenting and, finally, contemplate the rewards of our commitment.

A JOB DESCRIPTION FOR GRANDPARENTS (Part 7)

The simplicity of the program design is deceptive. Although an annual birthday meeting and an annual report are the focus of *The Business of Life,* the consultation will require the best of a whole collection of personnel and management skills, of childhood development knowledge, and of values, along with an honest view of the way the world really works day in and day out.

THE BIRTHDAY PROGRAM

> ### A JOB DESCRIPTION FOR GRANDPARENTS (Part 7)
>
> #### JOB CONTENT
>
> *The Business Of Life* consultant will be expected to facilitate the annual meeting. Both the knowledge and skills possessed by the individual entrepreneur will be realized during this regular event. The birthday conversations will consist of a review of the child's learning experiences during the past year with a view towards values clarification.
>
> The executive must willingly embrace the long-term potential of this ritual and not be discouraged by short-term difficulties.
>
> #### MONITORING AND MAINTENANCE
>
> Preparation of the annual report, titled *My Book of Birthdays*, is a requirement of the job. The contents should be available for subsequent annual meetings.
>
> The completed book may be given as a remembrance to the grandchild at the discretion of the grandparent.

(To be continued.)

PART NINE

THE BUSINESS OF LIFE

A belief in the value of a society's elders is not new. It is present today in most of the world's cultures. One vision for the next century in America says that grandparents will return to the family fold and play an integral part in a renewal of the traditional hierarchy. Some think that we may even live in intergenerational compounds where grandparents will serve as baby sitters for the young and as caregivers for aging parents. Grandparents could become the new educators by filling a role similar to that of ancient tribal elders. In this scenario, older generations would be valued once again for their wisdom and experience.[1]

Whatever may change, *The Business of Life* program gives us—here and now—a simple concept and a workable process by which we can hope to adapt and moderate the effects that modern lifestyles have on our grandchildren. It also gives us potential for the immediate creation of a new way to experience grandparenting.

"Maintenance is the reverse side of innovation," Gail Sheehy wrote in *Pathfinders*.[2] It is a reality that faces every entrepreneur. Over time, as you conduct *Birthday Program* consultations with your grandchildren, your skills and your dutiful record keeping will make it possible to review events in your grandchild's life, to appreciate the trial and error that every child must encounter, to share and remember the joy of those discoveries, and to reflect upon the rewards of learning. Each of us will look for expressions of *The Three C's* meaning good *character* values, demonstrations of *civility* in action, and instances that represent good *citizenship*, and, finding them, we will use the proper adult terminology as appropriate to the age of the grandchild. Throughout the years, after each birthday consultation is finished, we will complete a new page in *My Book of Birthdays*.

And, of course, no grandparent will ever forget the importance of smiles, laughter, and hugs!

CHAPTER 29. Working in the Real World

Nothing as complex as *The Business of Life* can ever be expected to flow as smoothly as this description would suggest. I am sure that you have already anticipated potential problems. I have experienced some and can imagine others.

Who Is Going to Fill the Consultant Role?

Until now I have been addressing each grandparent as an individual. However, unless you are divorced or a widow or widower, there are two grandparents at your house who may share equal devotion to a given grandchild. In this situation, depending on your own preferences, the two of you may want to share *The Business of Life* process and take turns conducting the birthday meetings. In this case, you will also want to share the preparation of the yearly summary and you will both need an ongoing understanding of the child's history.

Because this activity is strictly voluntary, I am inclined to expect that those of us, male or female, who have a natural tendency towards this sort of thing will emerge as the active entrepreneurs and that these individuals will provide continuity and follow-through for the duration. Still, there is no reason why couples should refrain from trying some creative solutions. My only doubt would be for the advisability of sharing a single consultation. That solution could overwhelm the child. It just feels too heavy-handed to me.

Still, if there are two of you who desire to participate, consider the following idea as a potential solution. Have you ever heard about or made use of *half-birthdays?* Sometimes when a child has a Christmas season birthday, for instance, the family chooses to have the party six months in between, or on the half-birthday, because in June there is time to give full attention to the celebration. You might want to use the half-birthday idea to solve *The Birthday Program* dilemma that will surface when both grandparents want to be involved, and it may be especially pertinent when there is only one grandchild in the family. Of course, this selection need not have any relationship to Christmas or a similar holiday. The point is to share the consultation without waiting for a full year by using the half-birthday of your grandchild whenever it occurs. In this variation, two consultations could be designed each year, one for each grandparent, by using the actual birthday and the half-birthday.

Another factor that may influence the choice between consultants involves the situation of mixing sexes as in a grandfather/granddaughter combination or vice versa. We would expect that this point will be pertinent during the years of adolescence. While there are certain subjects which call for male-to-male sensitivity or female-to-female understanding, it can also be helpful and enlightening to hear the views of the opposite sex. Of course, there is nothing in real life to prevent frequent talks between any of us and our grandchildren, and nothing about the *Business of Life* system should be interpreted so as to LIMIT substantive conversations to once a year!

What About Consultation Difficulties?

We need to be very realistic about an actual birthday party. Some of them are big productions! There may certainly be several grandparents and many other relatives in attendance, not to mention a group of active, noisy youngsters. Perhaps you have traveled a good distance to be there and you arrive tired. Maybe there is a daytime party for the children and an evening event for the family. This can be fun, but young children especially can be exhausted by the amount of unusual activity. Once it is clear to you that too many events are already scheduled, either conduct your consultation the day before the party or a day or two later.

A wise grandparent will choose a time and place according to circumstances. There is no sense in forcing the event to fit into a completely unsuitable situation. Quiet and privacy are best. Perhaps that will mean taking a walk or finding an unoccupied room. The timing needs to be such that you can expect of be free from interruptions. Neither should the child be anticipating the arrival of someone nor the beginning of some activity. Both of you should be calm and rested.

My own first experiment with this concept occurred several months after my grandchild's birthday because of the particular circumstances of my life in that period. No young child is likely to notice or to care. In time though, I would expect that our grandchildren will recognize this relationship and begin to equate their birthdays with the opportunity to have a special talk with Grandpa or Nana.

Of course, as mature adults, we must realize that the birthday talk may be condensed into a five-minute conversation when we begin the process with children in the four-to-seven-year range. But keep your entrepreneurial spirit alive! Remember that you are working on the strength of repetition and, as the children grow, more and more will become possible.

What About Different Points of View?

Is it necessary that grandparenting be a carbon copy of parenting? Certainly there are bound to be beliefs and practices which our grandchildren's parents prefer and believe in that we do not like one bit. The way you choose to deal with these differences is up to you. Please do recognize that I am not promoting confrontation with parents over child-raising methods. Even if you must tolerate parenting practices that you dislike, keep on creating your own private, regular conversations with your grandchild. Do not engage in any direct, disparaging remarks about your grandchild's parents—even if your grandchild needs to talk about those relationships. Our role is to support values and behaviors that we believe in and not to act as judge or jury when it comes to the parents. Actually, we should fully expect to have ideas and beliefs that are somewhat different than theirs due to our age, our experiences, and our mature judgement.

What If My Grandchild Refuses to Participate?

When you are dealing with a difficult client, one who is argumentative, Leland and Bailey suggest that you follow three rules. First, let the customer vent. In this case, the consultant listens patiently without protesting. Second, zip your lip. Don't interrupt or argue or attempt to explain your position. And third, don't take it personally.[1]

Just don't give up. This could be a good time to express empathy and to make use of your best interviewing skills in order to proceed. Or, if you feel it is warranted, you could simply cancel the consultation for the time being. Keep in mind, however, that a teenager may well intentionally test your staying power. Don't be too easily drawn in by this maneuver. This is a good time for a demonstration of wisdom and maturity—and staying power—on the part of a grandparent. Keep the L/B, (i.e., Leland and Bailey) mantra in your mind: let your client vent, keep your lips zipped, and don't take the outburst personally. Remember that this advice comes from professionals based on their own experiences.

Never doubt that paid consultants in the business world confront disagreements and outbursts of anger from their clients. The best consultants attempt to make use of the situation and to clarify the problem so that it can be addressed and resolved. The consultant, after all, is there to move things forward to a satisfactory conclusion. Keep that long-term goal in mind.

What Else Could Go Wrong?

At this stage of our lives, each of us knows that real life is unpredictable. Things rarely transpire as anticipated. And so we should be prepared to find that our eagerly expected payoff can be a long time in coming. Fortunately, this is a reality which shouldn't throw us off course nor should it raise serious doubt in our minds of the value of the effort. We are fully capable of patience and stubborn persistence when we *know* there is a long-term benefit to be gained. It is our supreme advantage in this *Business of Life*.

Will you experience the thrill of success on your first trial of this process? "No" is as likely as "yes." Despite our best efforts, we can surely expect a variety of responses from our grandchildren. If you feel that your consultation didn't work as well as you had hoped it would, re-examine your expectations. Do not be dismayed, but do think it over. Perhaps a little more homework is in order. Maybe you had such a good time that you completely forgot to notice any good values at all. Look for them in retrospect. It takes practice and preparation, so be realistic. Make a phone call later or drop by, if you can, and pose some follow-up questions to emphasize behaviors or values that you forgot to mention. The best advice might be to fashion an ideal in your mind's eye, but be prepared to compromise!

CHAPTER 30. Grandparents at Work

We often say, in this country, that children are our most important resource. This comment is regularly followed by disparaging remarks about our collective failure to act in ways that demonstrate a commitment to this belief. Our new-fashioned grandparenting business is a modern attempt to make full use of our knowledge, experience, and skills as we assist in the development of healthy, loving, competent, productive, and principled adults who will contribute to our society. Young adults who exhibit these characteristics will represent the outcome of a successful consulting venture in *The Business of Life*.

The Birthday Program sets the stage for our own creative interpretation of that tradition of the elders which is to guide and inspire new generations. On the face of it, this whole concept seems simple and, indeed, it is. It is in the execution of the idea that the challenge is hidden. It is the performance that holds the potential for change.

Even by creating the minimum, ritual birthday event you will find yourself involved in the reality of a focused kind of grandparenting. The extent to which you are committed, prepared, and conscientious about your performance will show in the kind of results that develop.

A planned and organized annual birthday meeting with its system of repetitive opportunities for meaningful conversation is one definition of *quality time*. While it isn't the sum total of what grandparenting is all about, it can be thought of as an essential part of the role. It's so much more meaningful than distant admiration of grandchildren and superficial contact.

If we grandparents fail to engage our grandchildren in talk and contemplation about real life, we may not be recognized as real people. Meaningful interaction with them shows that grandparents aren't just stagnant old folks. These consultations make our role seem purposeful. They signify an active involvement in everyday subjects that make a difference. We grandparents know about many things that are current and relevant. Being a grandparent is good and is something to look forward to. We need to be terrific role models for substantive grandparenting, so that we will be copied.

What happens after *The Birthday Program* has been completed and your grandchild is launched into young adulthood? You will always have a password in the phrase, "What did you discover this year?" You may have long since finished *My Book of Birthdays* and you may be 85 years old, but you can nonetheless still smile and pose that question. If you can parlay this birthday ritual into an open, trusting dialogue with a grandchild, you will have a wonderful treasure. You can still be relevant and you can always listen. Never mind your ailments. Just ask good, open-ended questions and you will still be very much involved in the real life of your adult grandchildren. Think of it: a lifelong relationship between the two of you, based on the freedom and confidence needed to engage in serious conversation about things that matter and shared things that you both remember.

The idea that we elders should *consciously* contribute to the perpetuation of our cultural conscience is one whose time has come. By adopting a new definition of grandparenting, a description that calls for action, we have reason to stay healthy, informed, and young.

In a philosophical sense, *The Business of Life* represents our need and our drive to replicate and replace ourselves through our progeny even as we know that they must evolve in a new world. It is when we take care of that responsibility as a society that we truly have a hand in creating the future.

THE BUSINESS OF LIFE

Common sense suggests that only a few of our conversations will have a particularly memorable impact. It is simply true that our efforts will be only a part of the child's reality, and we may never receive recognition for teaching specific lessons. Yet, consider the overall impact for a moment. Remember the symbol you will represent of the role every grandparent should play in life. Keep in mind the simple certainty that paying attention to a child while reinforcing good values and good habits will help to mold that child into a thoughtful, confident, and competent adult.

As you put your franchise into operation, keep these things in mind. All of us who are *Business of Life* grandparents, as a group, share the following:

- We believe in the importance of individual character, shared civility, and the requirements of citizenship.
- We support the habit of self-evaluation or reflection for ourselves and our grandchildren.
- We know that the process of learning is more important than awards.
- We can identify the values shown in a grandchild's words and deeds.
- We practice the art of proactive listening.
- We have the expertise needed for the delivery of quality, professional consulting.
- We are committed to *The Business of Life* process and to excellence in grandparenting.
- We intend to be leaders in the creation of a new grandparent/ grandchild ritual.

And finally, each of us will be actively involved in training another set of future grandparents. Many of us will eventually know that a new series of annual birthday meetings can be expected to take place with yet another, new generation. What a lovely legacy.

A COMPLETE JOB DESCRIPTION FOR *THE BUSINESS OF LIFE*

JOB POSTING

Please be advised that the following employment opportunity is now available.

BUSINESS OF LIFE GRANDPARENT

EXECUTIVE PROFILE

The successful applicant will be self-motivated, enthusiastic, confident, and will possess an entrepreneurial spirit. The inner drive to accomplish long-term goals is imperative and the enjoyment of young children is essential. This mature adult will want to share the important lessons of life and help guide a new generation of American youngsters by interacting one-on-one with his or her own grandchildren.

JOB CONTENT

Active research and information gathering will support professional results. Awareness of social issues and the daily environment of each grandchild forms the background for skillful consulting.

An appreciation of fundamental American values is necessary. This may require some active review of values application in the areas of character, civility, and citizenship. An ability to recognize the expression of values through the behaviors of youngsters will maximize results.

Every practitioner must agree in principle with the mission statement and be ready to put it into practice.

A comfortable familiarity with modern leadership concepts must be demonstrated and applicable management skills must be sharpened for successful implementation of the mission if necessary, remedial exercises may be required.

Possession of a good understanding of the learning capabilities of children at various stages of development will guide the committed grandparent in content and delivery style.

The highest level of excellence in customer service shall be the goal of every consultant.

The Business of Life consultant will be expected to facilitate the annual meeting. Bot the knowledge and skills possessed by the individual entrepreneur will be realized during this regular event. The birthday conversations will consist of a review of the child's learning experiences during the past year with a view towards values clarification.

The executive must willingly embrace the long-term potential of this ritual and not be discouraged by short-term difficulties.

MONITORING AND MAINTENANCE

Preparation of the annual report, titled *My Book of Birthdays,* is a requirement of the job. The contents should be available for subsequent annual meetings.

The completed book may be given as a remembrance to the grandchild at the discretion of the grandparent.

JOB BENEFITS

Every grandparent who embarks on *The Business of Life* can expect to achieve the personal satisfaction of a job well done. You will have fulfilled a responsibility of life and you will have the pleasure of a true relationship with your grandchildren.

Appendices

REFERENCES

Part 1

1. Hillary Johnson, "Retirement Special: Boom Years," *Worth* (April 1998), 54.

Chapter 1

1. Ken Dychtwald and Joe Flower, *Age Wave: The Challenges and Opportunities of an Aging America* (Los Angeles: Jeremy P. Tarcher, 1989), 344.
2. Dychtwald and Flower, *Age Wave*, 6.
3. Dychtwald and Flower, *Age Wave*, 273.
4. Arthur Kornhaber and Kenneth L. Woodward, *Grandparents/Grandchildren* (Garden City: Anchor Press, 1981).
5. Fitzhugh Dodson and Paula Reuben, *How to Grandparent* (New York: Harper and Row, 1981).
6. Jerry Gerber, Janet Wolff, Walter Klores, and Gene Brown, *Lifetrends: The Future of Baby Boomers and Other Aging Americans* (New York: Stonesong Press, 1989), 3.
7. Gail Sheehy, *New Passages: Mapping Your Life Across Time* (New York: Random House, 1995), 139.
8. Dychtwald and Flower, *Age Wave,* 344.
9. Sharan B. Merriam and Rosemary S. Caffarella, *Learning in Adulthood: A Comprehensive Guide.* (San Francisco: Jossey-Bass, 1991), 198.
10. Merriam and Caffarella, *Learning in Adulthood,* 198

Chapter 2

1. Fitzhugh Dodson and Paula Reuben, *How to Grandparent* (New York: Harper and Row, 1981), 121.
2. Stephen R. Covey, *The Seven Habits of Highly Effective Families* (New York: Golden Books, 1997).
3. Arthur Kornhaber and Kenneth L. Woodward, *Grandparents/Grandchildren* (Garden City: Anchor Press, 1981).
4. Lois Wyse, *Funny, You Don't Look Like a Grandmother* (New York: Crown, 1989).
5. T. Berry Brazelton, *Touchpoints: Your Child's Emotional and Behavioral Development, the Essential Reference* (Reading: Addison-Wesley, 1992), 430.

NEW-FASHIONED GRANDPARENTING

6. Stephanie Coontz, *The Way We Never Were: American Families and the Nostalgia Trap* (New York: Basic Books, 1992), 33–5.
7. James Lincoln Collier, *The Rise of Selfishness in America* (New York: Oxford University Press, 1991), 262.

Chapter 3

1. Hillary Rodham Clinton, *It Takes a Village; and Other Lessons Children Teach Us* (New York: Simon and Schuster, 1996), 314–5.

Part 2

1. Sam Roberts, *Who We Are: A Portrait of America Based on the Latest United States Census* (New York: Times Books, 1993), 220.
2. Fiona Soltis, "Listen If Teen Talks Suicide," *The Tennessean,* June 29, 1998, sec. D, p. 6.

Part 3

Chapter 6

1. John P. Dworetzky, *Introduction to Child Development,* 2d ed. (St Paul: West Publishing, 1984), 407.
2. Stephanie Coontz, *The Way We Really Are: Coming to Terms with America's Changing Families* (New York: Basic Books, 1997), 13, 28.
3. Grace Palladino, *Teenagers: An American History* (New York: Basic Books, 1996), xv.
4. Palladino, *Teenagers: An American History*, xiv–xviii.
5. David Elkind, *Parenting Your Teenager in the 90's: Practical Information and Advice About Adolescent Development and Contemporary Issues* (Rosemont: Modern Learning Press, 1993), iv–vi.
6. David J. Schneider, *Introduction to Social Psychology* (San Diego: Harcourt Brace Jovanovich, 1988), 280.

Chapter 8

1. Laura Schlessinger, *How Could You Do That?!* (New York: HarperCollins, 1996), 72.

Part 4

1. Matthew McKay and Patrick Fanning, *Self-Esteem: A Proven Program of Cognitive Techniques for Assessing and Improving and Maintaining Your Self-Esteem,* 2d ed. (Oakland: New Harbinger, 1992), 100–2.

References

Chapter 8

1. Robert N. Bellah, et al., *The Good Society* (New York: Vintage Books, 1992), 180.
2. Gerald F. Cavanagh, *American Business Values*, 2d ed. (Englewood Cliffs: Prentice-Hall, 1984), 26
3. Cavanagh, *American Business Values*. 2d ed., 19.
4. Cavanagh, *American Business Values*. 2d ed., 19.
5. Cavanagh, *American Business Values*. 2d ed., 20, 22.
6. Cavanagh, *American Business Values*. 2d ed., 20, 21.
7. Cavanagh, *American Business Values*. 2d ed., 23, 26.

Chapter 9

1. Michael L. Loren, *The Road to Virtue* (New York: Avon Books, 1996), 3–5.
2. Daniel Goleman, *Emotional Intelligence: Why It Can Matter More than IQ* (New York: Bantam, 1997).
3. Goleman, *Emotional Intelligence*, 285.
4. Benjamin M. Spock, *A Better World for Our Children: Rebuilding American Family Values* (Chicago: Contemporary Books, 1996), 20.
5. Lillian Carson, *The Essential Grandparent: A Guide to Making a Difference* (Deerfield Beach: Health Communications, 1996), 208.

Chapter 10

1. Jerome Kagan, *The Nature of the Child* (New York: Basic Books, 1984), 147–8.
2. Neil Postman, *The Disappearance of Childhood* (New York: Delacorte Press, 1982), 87.
3. Postman, *The Disappearance of Childhood*, 88.
4. William J. Bennett, ed., *The Book of Virtues: A Treasury of the World's Great Moral Stories* (New York: Simon and Schuster, 1993), 14.
5. Robert Bly, *The Sibling Society* (New York: Vintage Books, 1977), 48.
6. Deborah Tannen, *The Argument Culture: Moving from Debate to Dialogue* (New York: Random House, 1998), 25.

Chapter 11

1. Laura Schlessinger, *How Could You Do That?!* (New York: HarperCollins, 1996), 93.

2. Phil Catalfo, *Raising Spiritual Children in a Material World; Introducing Spirituality into Family Life* (New York: Berkley Books, 1997), 238.

3. Catalfo, *Raising Spiritual Children in a Material World*, 239.

4. Richard Carlson, *Don't Sweat the Small Stuff…and It's All Small Stuff: Simple Ways to Keep the Little Things from Taking over Your Life* (New York: Hyperion, 1997), 193.

5. Letitia Baldridge, *More Than Manners: Raising Today's Kids to Have Kind Manners and Good Hearts* (New York: Rawson Associates, 1997), 58.

Part 5

Chapter 13

1. Roger E. Allen, *Winnie-the-Pooh on Management; In Which a Very Important Bear and His Friends Are Introduced to a Very Important Subject* (New York: Penguin Group, 1994).

2. Wess Roberts and Bill Ross, *Make It So: Leadership Lessons from Star Trek: The Next Generation* (New York: Pocket Books, 1995).

3. Peter Block, *Flawless Consulting: A Guide to Getting Your Expertise Used* (San Diego: Pfeiffer, 1986), 1.

4. Block, *Flawless Consulting*, 4, 5.

5. Saturn Corporation. *Leadership at Saturn* (a brochure) Spring Hill, TN.

6. Ken Blanchard and Don Shula, *Everyone's a Coach; You Can Inspire Anyone to Be a Winner* (New York: Zondervan Publishing House and Harper Business, 1995), 29.

7. Jeffery Zaslow, "Straight Talk," *USA Weekend* (January 30–February 1, 1998), 14.

8. William Hendricks, ed., *Coaching, Mentoring and Managing* (Franklin Lakes, NJ: Career Press, 1996), 128.

Chapter 14

1. Ester Wachs Book, "Leadership for the Millenium," *Working Woman* (March 1998), 29.

2. Sunny Baker and Kim Baker, *The Complete Idiot's Guide to Project Management* (New York: Alpha Books, 1998), 14–8.

References

Chapter 15

1. James P Womack and Daniel T. Jones, *Lean Thinking: Banish Waste and Create Wealth in Your Corporation* (New York: Simon and Schuster, 1996), 15.

2. Womack and Jones, *Lean Thinking*, 24.

3. Womack and Jones, *Lean Thinking*, 23.

4. Lee Bolman and Terrance Deal, *Reframing Organizations; Artistry, Choice, and Leadership* (San Francisco: Jossey-Bass, 1991), Introduction.

Part 6

Chapter 16

1. Mel Silberman, *Active Training: A Handbook of Techniques, Designs, Case Examples, and Tips* (New York: Lexington Books, 1990), 1–3.

2. John P Dworetzky, *Introduction to Child Development*, 2d ed. (St Paul: West Publishing, 1984).

3. James W. Vander Zanden, *Human Development*, 3d ed. (New York: Alfred Knopf, 1995).

4. Howard Gardner, *Multiple Intelligences: The Theory in Practice* (New York: Basic Books, 1993), 8.

5. William Hendricks, ed., *Coaching, Mentoring and Managing* (Franklin Lakes: Career Press, 1996), 66.

Chapter 17

1. Melvin Konner, *Childhood* (Boston: Little, Brown, 1991), 242.

2. John P. Dworetzky, *Introduction to Child Development*, 2d ed. (St Paul: West Publishing, 1984), 314.

3. Konner, *Childhood*, 298–9.

4. Madeline Levine, *Viewing Violence: How Media Violence Affects Your Child and Adolescent* (New York: Doubleday, 1996), 130–1.

5. Robert Fulghum, *All I Really Need to Know I Learned in Kindergarten* (New York: Ivy Books, 1986), 3–6.

Chapter 18

1. Melvin Konner, *Childhood* (Boston: Little, Brown, 1991), 326–7.

2. Melvin Konner, *Childhood* (Boston: Little, Brown, 1991), 327.

3. Lawrence Kutner, *Your School-Age Child* (New York: William Morrow, 1996), 40.

4. Stanley I. Greenspan, *Playground Politics: Understanding the Emotional Life of Your School-Age Child* (Reading: Addison-Wesley, 1993), 16.

Chapter 19

1. Madeline Levine, *Viewing Violence: How Media Violence Affects Your Child and Adolescent* (New York: Doubleday, 1996), 174.
2. Levine, *Viewing Violence*, 166.
3. Levine, *Viewing Violence*, 163–4.
4. Robert Coles, *The Moral Intelligence of Children: How to Raise a Moral Child* (New York: Plume, 1998), 162.
5. Fitzhugh Dodson and Paula Reuben, *How to Grandparent* (New York: Harper and Row, 1981), 94–6.
6. Melvin Konner, *Childhood* (Boston: Little, Brown, 1991), 354.
7. Konner, *Childhood*, 355.
8. Jerome Kagan, *The Nature of the Child* (New York: Basic Books, 1984, 273–4.

Chapter 20

1. Melvin Konner, *Childhood* (Boston: Little, Brown, 1991), 387-8.
2. Grace Palladino, *Teenagers: An American History* (New York: Basic Books, 1996), 256.
3. Palladino, *Teenagers*, 258–9.
4. Margot Hornblower, "Great Expectations," *Time* [Latin American Edition] (June 9, 1997), 38–46.
5. Robert Owen, *Gen X TV: "The Brady Bunch" to "Melrose Place"* (New York: Syracuse University Press, 1997), 2.
6. Hornblower, "Great Expectations," 38–46.
7. Owen, *Gen X TV*, 11.
8. Owen, *Gen X TV*, 210–1.

Chapter 22

1. Wayne W. Dyer, *What Do You Really Want for Your Children?* (New York: Avon Books, 1985), 379.
2. Elizabeth Fenwick and Tony Smith, *Adolescence: The Survival Guide for Parents and Teenagers* (New York: DK Publishing, 1996), 242.
3. Fiona Soltis, "Listen If Teen Talks Suicide," *The Tennessean*, June 29, 1998, sec. D, p. 8.

References

4. Soltis, "Listen If Teen Talks Suicide," 8.

5. Dick Schaaf, *Keeping the Edge: Giving Customers the Service They Demand* (New York: Penguin, 1995), 316.

6. Schaaf, *Keeping the Edge*, 24.

7. Charles E. Schaefer, *How to Influence Children: A Handbook of Practical Child Guidance Skills*, 2d ed. (Northvale, NJ: Jason Aronson, 1994), 243.

8. Dale Carnegie, *How to Win Friends and Influence People* (New York: Simon and Schuster, 1981), 81–94.

9. Richard C. Whiteley, *The Customer-Driven Company* (Reading: Addison-Wesley, 1991), 46.

10. Kim H. Krisco, *Leadership and the Art of Conversation* (Rocklin, CA: Prima Publishing, 1997), 166–7.

11. Schaefer, *How to Influence Children*, 242.

12. Schaefer, *How to Influence Children*, 242.

13. Schaefer, *How to Influence Children*, 258.

14. Judy Blume, *Letters to Judy: What Your Kids Wish They Could Tell You* (New York: G.P. Putnam's Sons, 1986), 11, 14.

15. William Pollack, *Real Boys: Rescuing Our Sons from the Myth of Boyhood* (New York: Random House, 1989), 20.

16. Haim G. Ginott, *Between Parent and Child: New Solutions to Old Problems* (New York: Macmillan, 1965), 74.

17. Stanley Greenspan, *Playground Politics: Understanding the Emotional Life of Your School-Age Child* (Reading: Addison-Wesley, 1993), 92.

18. Karen Leland and Keith Bailey, *Customer Service for Dummies* (Foster City: IDG Worldwide, 1995), 244.

19. Krisco, *Leadership*, 162.

Chapter 23

1. Lawrence Kutner, *Your School-Age Child* (New York: William Morrow, 1996), 112–3.

2. Kutner, *Your School-Age Child*, 113.

3. Alfie Kohn, *Punished by Rewards* (Boston: Houghton Mifflin, 1993), 97.

4. Kohn, *Punished by Rewards*, 101.

5. Kohn, *Punished by Rewards*, 102.

6. Kohn, *Punished by Rewards*, 108–9.

7. Barbara Unell and Jerry L. Wyckoff, *20 Teachable Virtues: Practical Ways to Pass on Lessons of Virtue and Character to Your Children* (New York: Berkley Publishing Group, 1995), 20.

8. Kohn, *Punished by Rewards*, 35.

9. Kohn, *Punished by Rewards*, 53.

10. Stephanie Marston, *The Magic of Encouragement: Nurturing Your Child's Self-Esteem* (New York: Pocket Books, 1990), 98.

11. Dale Carnegie, *How to Win Friends and Influence People* (New York: Simon and Schuster, 1981), 251.

12. Carnegie, *How to Win Friends and Influence People*, 237.

13. Carnegie, *How to Win Friends and Influence People*, 237

14. David Elkind, *Parenting Your Teenager in the 90's: Practical Information and Advice About Adolescent Development and Contemporary Issues* (Rosemont: Modern Learning Press, 1993), 113.

15. Marston, *The Magic of Encouragement*, 98.

Chapter 24

1. Lee Bolman and Terrance Deal, *Reframing Organizations: Artistry, Choice, and Leadership* (San Francisco: Jossey-Bass, 1991), 299.

2. Joseph Campbell and Bill Moyers, *The Power of Myth* (New York: Doubleday, 1988), 8.

3. Campbell and Moyers, *The Power of Myth*, 8.

4. Evan Imber-Black and Janine Roberts, eds. *Rituals for Our Times: Celebrating, Healing, and Changing Our Lives and Our Relationships* (New York: Harper Perennial, 1993), 3.

5. Campbell and Moyers, *The Power of Myth*, 83.

6. Campbell and Moyers, *The Power of Myth*, 8, 83.

7. Imber-Black and Roberts, *Rituals for Our Times*, 3.

Chapter 27

1. Debora Phillips, *How to Give Your Child a Great Self-Image: Proven Techniques to Build Confidence from Infancy to Adolescence* (New York: Random House, 1989), 59.

2. Judy Blume, *Letters to Judy: What Your Kids Wish They Could Tell You* (New York: G.P. Putnam's Sons, 1986), 153.

Part 9

1. Gerald Celente, *Trends 2000: How to Prepare for and Profit from the Changes of the 21st Century* (New York: Warner Books, 1997), 235–6.
2. Gail Sheehy, *Pathfinders* (New York: William Morrow, 1981), 475.

Chapter 30

1. Karen Leland and Keith Bailey, *Customer Service for Dummies* (Foster City: IDG Worldwide, 1995), 240.

INDEX

aphorisms, 165, 204, 215, 216

Baby Boomers, 14, 15, 50, 193
Bennett, William, 87
Blume, Judy, 166, 213, 214
Brazelton, T. Berry, M.D., 21

Campbell, Joseph, 189, 191
Carnegie, Dale, 161, 163, 180, 181
coaching, 109, 110, 112, 113, 114, 181
cognitive development, 131, 132, 133, 136, 145
confidentiality, 157, 158, 161, 195, 201
consulting skills, 195
Covey, Stephen, 20
cultural norm, 54, 55, 56
customer service, 152, 155 156, 159, 177, 180

Dagara, 5

emotional intelligence, 79
empathy, 18, 51, 78, 89, 161, 170, 171, 177, 200, 213, 225

Generation X, 148, 149, 150
generativity, 18
Ginott, Dr. Haim, 168
guilt, 85, 95, 96, 140

IMAGINE: Exercise, 28, 59, 106, 119, 159, 209
interviewing skills, 116, 117, 119, 120, 225
Kohn, Alfie, 173, 174, 179
Kornhaber, Dr. Arthur, 11, 20

lean thinking, 121, 122, 123
letter writing, 213, 214, 215
listening, art of, 161, 163, 218

Index

management skills, 100
market research, 61, 129
mentoring, 109, 113, 181
Mission Statement, 8, 100, 101, 125

Piaget, Jean, 132, 146
proactive listening, 227
project management, 36
project manager, 114, 115

REMINDER, 31, 39, 112, 162, 197, 201

Santa Claus, 136
Schlessinger, Dr. Laura, 57, 92
self-image, 10, 85, 205
shame, 85, 86, 87, 161
Sheehy, Gail, 13, 17, 221
situation ethics, 78, 149
spirituality, 80
suicide, 157, 158

virtues, 77, 87

wisdom, definition of, 18, 19

MAIL ORDER INFORMATION

To order more copies of

✔ New-Fashioned Grandparenting

contact: BookMasters, Inc.
P.O. Box 388
Ashland, OH 44805

by phone (800) 247–6553

by E-mail: order@bookmaster.com

by FAX: (419) 281–6883

Please inquire about the availability of the album

✔ My Book of Birthdays

Thank you for your order!

You are most welcome to contact the author, Julia Nelson, in care of the publisher.

Allyn Group Publications
P.O. Box 1116
Deleware, OH 43015-8116